Beer
and Brewing

**Dave Laing and
John Hendra**

Macdonald Guidelines

Contents

© Macdonald Educational Ltd. 1977

First published 1977
Macdonald Educational Ltd.
Holywell House,
Worship Street,
London, EC2A 2EN.

ISBN 0 356 06009 8

What is beer?

According to the dictionaries, beer is an "alcoholic liquor derived from fermented malt, flavoured with hops", but over the centuries it has been described in many ways. A certain Roman emperor wrote that "wine smells of nectar, but beer smells of goat". Later religious reformers and temperance supporters had even harsher words to say about beer and its intoxicating effect, though they have always been out-numbered by the poems and songs in praise of the drink.

The basic ingredient of beer is barley, one of the earliest cultivated crops, and the drink can trace its ancestry back to the time when man the hunter became man the farmer. According to the archaeologists, at least 40 per cent of the barley crop of Mesopotamia, the "fertile crescent" of the Middle East, was used for brewing in 3000 BC. It seems likely that beer-making arose as an accidental by-product of the earliest forms of baking. Malt bread is still sometimes called "beer bread".

For many centuries, beer was the staple drink of ordinary people all over Northern Europe. There were sound medical reasons for the popularity of the drink. The boiling and fermentation processes rendered it virtually germ-free, unlike the untreated drinking water of the time. Beer was also a central feature of ceremonial events. Viking warriors drank to their success out of massive two-handled cups before setting out on their raids. In more peaceful times, special ales were brewed for christenings and weddings.

The beer of those days was almost cer-tainly sweeter and stronger than the drink we know in modern times, mainly because it did not include hops. This ingredient only came into general use about 500 years ago, but apart from that brewing today is fundamentally the same as in Roman times. Technological advances have increased the speed and efficiency of brewing, but the four stages of malting, mashing, boiling and fermentation are still essential to the process.

Brewing at home

Malting and mashing prepare the barley grains for conversion into alcohol, boiling releases the resins and oils in the hops to provide the flavour, while during fermenta-tion, yeast does its work to produce the finished alcoholic drink. With the correct equipment, much of which may already be to hand, the home brewer can carry out these activities to make a beer that will compare favourably with the varieties produced on a large scale in modern commercial breweries.

In fact, by brewing at home, the beer enthusiast is able to experiment with different quantities of the various ingre-dients, and various ways of carrying out the essential processes, to make a brew that suits his own palate. The commercial brewer, on the other hand, is constrained by the demands of mass-production to choose the cheapest raw materials and to stick to the same strength and flavour in every brew.

▶ The ripe ear of barley is the basic ingredient of beer. 80 per cent of barley by weight consists of starch, which is converted to sugar by malting and mashing, and to alcohol by fermentation.

Bygone brewing

The first large-scale brewing industry grew up in Ancient Egypt. The beer, called *hek*, was sweet-tasting and flavoured with mandrake, not hops. Egyptian beer-drinking was the preserve of the lower classes. The aristocracy preferred wine and tried to curb the popularity of *hek* by closing down the shops which sold it. Their job was finally done for them by the Arab armies which conquered Egypt during the 8th century AD. As followers of Mohammed and his sacred book, the Koran, they were opposed to alcohol in any form, as the Moslem faith still is today.

Elsewhere in the Middle East, beer-like drinks were common. The Jews made a brew called *sicera,* probably from a recipe learned during their captivity in Egypt. It was said to have protected them from leprosy during their exile in Babylon, another ancient civilization with its own fermented drink. In Western Asia, at the same period, *koumiss*, an intoxicating brew made from mares' milk, was widely known.

Just over 2000 years ago, the centre of beer production shifted from the Middle East to Northern Europe. The earliest accounts of beers in this area came from the historians of the Roman Empire, though it is likely that knowledge of beer-making from fermented barley had arrived with the Phoenicians, a trading and sea-faring people from North Africa.

The tribes of Northern Germany, as well as the Spaniards and the British, had a brew flavoured with honey which the wine-drinking Romans viewed with disdain. One of their chroniclers described the drink as "a compound of bad juices which does harm to the muscles". This is possibly the

▲ An Egyptian brewer at work. The malt was dried by baking into beer cakes before mashing took place in large clay vessels.

first recorded reference to the symptoms of a hangover!

The Romans, however, introduced the custom of providing special places for drinking. Their *tabernae* were the forerunners of today's bars and taverns. These buildings were placed at regular intervals along the straight roads which ran the length of the Empire. Originally, they were bleak lodging-houses providing the bare necessities of food and drink for travellers, but they gradually became places of relaxation and entertainment.

Brewing monks

Brewing survived the collapse of the Roman Empire, just as it had preceded it. By the time of the Middle Ages there was a well-established "frontier" between the beer and wine drinking areas of Europe. It ran roughly along the River Loire in France, then north of Champagne and over the Vosges into Germany where Bavaria, along with Bohemia (part of present day Czechoslovakia) was the heartland of brewing.

By now, monasteries had replaced the old *tabernae* as the centres of hospitality for the traveller and most skilled brewers were monks. Beer was established as the staple beverage of all sections of the population, rich and poor, men, women and children. It was commonplace for large amounts of beer to be consumed with every meal (at some monasteries, the brothers were allowed a gallon a day) and the breweries grew in size and output. Fountains Abbey, in Northern England, was capable of producing 360 gallons at one time.

By this time, water power was widely used for baking and brewing. At Clairvaux Abbey, in France, an ingenious system used the nearby river for power to grind corn and prepare flour, as well as providing water for beer. Soft water was regarded as the best liquor for brewing at this period.

The alewife

Among the ordinary people, most families still made their own beer, though brewing had also become a specialized trade. Just as the housewife was responsible for home-brewed ale, the village brewer was often a woman, the alewife. Her alehouse or tavern became a centre of village life, in competition with the church. To distinguish the alehouse from the surrounding cottages, a long pole was set up outside it. If wine was also sold, an evergreen bush was hung at the end of the pole.

The alewife was not always a highly regarded member of the village community. Severe penalties were prescribed for the brewing of bad ale, often involving the use of the ducking stool in the local pond.

The hop revolution

The method of brewing in Northern Europe remained unchanged from Roman times up until the 15th century. The standard German brew was *gruit* beer, flavoured with a mixture of herbs including bog myrtle, rosemary and yarrow. In other countries different herbs were used, but in general the standard beer was a strong, sweet drink.

The brewing revolution which took

▼ The alewife, in her elegant hat, appeared frequently in medieval engravings and church carvings.

7

place during the 15th and 16th centuries, starting in Germany, involved the replacement of these various flavourings by a new ingredient; hops. As well as giving the beer a more bitter taste, hops acted as a preservative, allowing it to be stored for longer periods than before. The use of hops, and their cultivation as an important crop, spread slowly from Germany to Holland and Belgium and then further north.

The introduction of the new beer encountered much opposition from drinkers of traditional unhopped varieties. In many places attempts were made to ban the use of hops in beer by law. One English writer warned his fellow-countrymen that drinking hopped beer would "kill those troubled with gall-stones and colic, or else make you fat and inflate the belly, as you can see from Dutchmen's faces and bellies".

Nevertheless, beer made with hops became accepted all over Europe, while in many countries bottom-fermented beer replaced the top-fermentation process. Originating in Bavaria in the 16th century, this beer came to be known as lager, after the German term for storage and was kept for a long time before drinking to allow a secondary fermentation to take place.

The scientific age

The 18th century was the age of the Industrial Revolution and brewing, like every other industry, was affected by the scientific discoveries of the time. Previously the power source for breweries had come from water mills or horse mills, in which one or more animals provided the energy to grind malt and pump water. Now, horse mills were replaced by steam engines and very soon only cotton and coal used more steam power than the breweries.

More profound changes were to follow. For centuries, the art of brewing had hardly changed. Secrets and traditions were handed

▲ Hop-picking by hand in the 16th century. Similar equipment was used until the recent introduction of machinery.

▶ A brewery scene in 1821. The figure at the top is stoking the fire under the copper.

BEER AND THE LAW
The most famous law to regulate the purity of beer is the German *Reinheitsgebot* passed in 1519 which is still in force today. It states that only barley malt, water and hops are to be used in brewing. Adulteration of beer was widespread as the price of malt and hops rose. Unscrupulous brewers added substances such as molasses, liquorice, opium, tobacco and sulphuric acid to the brew.

The strangest method of testing the strength of beer occurred in the Middle Ages. Wearing leather breeches, the official would sit on a bench covered in ale. If the breeches stuck to it, the beer was passed as strong enough.

on from father to son, involving methods that came to seem outdated in an age of scientific precision. To test the temperature of the hot water in the mash tun before adding the malt, the traditional brewer would swirl the water about with his finger. If he could bear the heat for long enough to repeat the movement three times, he would conclude that the right temperature had been reached. An alternative method was to wait until the water had cooled sufficiently for the brewer to see his face in it.

All this was no longer necessary once the thermometer, originally a purely scientific instrument, had been adapted for industrial use. Further precision was brought to brewing by the introduction of the hydrometer during the 18th century. This invention, now familiar to commercial and home brewers alike, measured the specific gravity of the brew. The sugar content of the beer could then be calculated and the brewer could judge whether it would be of the required strength after fermentation.

A third important innovation in the manufacture of beer at this period was the addition of finings to the fermented brew to dispel any remaining cloudiness. The most usual source of finings was isinglass, a substance extracted from the swim bladder of the sturgeon which at first was imported into Northern Europe from Russia. The need for fining beer became more urgent as the old pewter tankards were replaced by glass containers which made it possible for customers in the taverns to take a good look at what they were drinking!

The birth of modern brewing

As breweries grew in size during the 19th century, mechanization was introduced into processes which had previously been carried out by hand. Mechanical rakes were used for mashing, while sparging (the rinsing of the fermentable sugar from the malt), was made more efficient by a machine which sprayed streams of water onto the mash. To cope with the vast quantities of beer produced at each brew, stone vats were installed in the cellar of the brewery as an alternative to the old wooden casks.

▼ A 19th century mash tun with mechanical masher supplementing mashing by hand.

▼ Malting in the 19th century. Rootlets and other foreign matter are separated from freshly kilned malted grains.

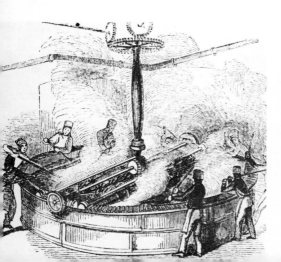

Sometimes brewers were over-ambitious, and there was at least one fatal accident when a giant vat burst.

Advances in the techniques of cooling and refrigeration also greatly assisted the expansion of the brewing trade. In earlier times, the making of beer in the hot weather of summer had always been a risky business, especially when bottom-fermented lager had to be kept at a low temperature.

Attemperation was the name given to the method by which pipes containing cold water were submerged in the fermenting beer to ensure that it cooled efficiently, even in the warmest climate. Ice machines were also now available to keep finished beer cool for months.

Better cooling also helped to cut down the risk of infection of the brew by bacteria, which could contaminate the brew on its way from the copper to the fermentation vessel. But there still remained one uncontrolled factor in the brewing process, which was liable to spoil the most carefully prepared beer: the yeast.

▲ Chandler & Co.'s brewery in London in 1893. The building shows typical brewery architecture of this time.

Louis Pasteur

The discovery of how yeast works as the active ingredient in the fermentation process was made by the great French scientist, Louis Pasteur. He had worked at first on wine, but later applied his knowledge to beer. By examining a batch of yeast before it was pitched into the wort, Pasteur could detect the presence of any malignant bacteria. Soon, every major brewery had installed a microscope and applied Pasteur's theories.

The work of Pasteur and other 19th century inventors forged the final link in the chain which led from the earliest brewers of Mesopotamia and Egypt to the large-scale automated commercial breweries which produce today's beer on a worldwide scale.

Modern commercial brewing

Brewing today is dominated, like any other industry, by the need to increase efficiency and expand production. And, at first sight, a modern brewery looks like any other factory designed for mass production. But the basic processes of brewing—malting, mashing, boiling and fermentation—are still necessary, whether the beer is made in the corner of the kitchen or a multi-million dollar block of concrete and steel.

Much of modern brewing technology is concerned with speeding up the various stages of beer-making, with the ultimate aim of a continuous brew in which all the

▲ Photomicrograph of barley.

▼ Barley being harvested by combine harvester.

plant is in constant use. Almost the only area in which such scientific ingenuity has not made much headway is the growing of beer's most substantial ingredients, grain and hops.

Barley

By far the most important grain for the brewer is barley, although maize or rice can be substituted and both are often added to the barley malt to make specific varieties of beer.

The barley crop is harvested some three months after sowing and stored for six weeks before being sent for malting. The main varieties of the cereal are known as two, four and six-row barley, according to the number of spikelets on either side of the ear. Four-row barley generally produces inferior grain and is not often used in brewing. A good malting barley must be undamaged, have plump grains and should not have undergone premature germination. If it contains too much nitrogen, the resulting beer will be of poor quality. Dark barley is used in the brewing of stouts, while lighter coloured grains are suitable for lager and bitter.

Preparing the hops

Unlike barley, which is a staple food crop, hop cultivation is determined solely by the needs of the brewer. Hops provide the bitter flavour of the finished beer and also act as a preservative.

The hop is a perennial climbing plant which grows to a height of six metres. In the winter, the climbing part (or bine) dies away, but the roots remain alive in the soil. At one time, sticks were provided for the plants to climb, but nowadays strings are connected to an overhead network of wire. The harvesting of the cones, which contain the hop flowers used in brewing, was previously done by hand when the whole bine would be pulled down and the cones picked off. Now the bine is completely severed before being taken off to the picking machine which uses hooks to strip the cones.

Most beer-producing countries produce seedless hops, using only female plants.

In Britain, by tradition, both male and female hops are grown and the resulting flowers are seeded. In general, seedless hops contain greater amounts of essential oils and resins, while the seeded variety grow more luxuriantly.

Once picked, the hop flowers must be dried, since the crop has to supply the brewery for a whole year. Modern methods using hot air from oil-fired furnaces beneath the floor of the drying chamber have reduced the drying time to ten hours. After drying, the hops are tightly baled and stored under refrigerated conditions, until required for beer-making.

▼ Harvesting the hops. Compare these contemporary hand-pickers with the 16th century technique on page 8.

At the maltings

Before brewing can begin, the barley grains must be converted into malt. This involves speeding up the natural process of growth during which the starch and protein inside the grain is converted into more soluble forms.

After the barley has been cleaned and graded, it is steeped in water until it swells by about a third in bulk. Next it goes to the malting floor where it is spread out to a depth of 10 cm and left to germinate, being turned occasionally. Traditionally, this process took up to ten days, but in their search for greater productivity some modern brewers cut down the germination time to as little as four days by the addition of gibberellic acid, which speeds up the activity of the barley grains.

The germination process of this green malt, as it is called, is halted by drying in a hot kiln. The temperature varies according to the type of beer to be made. Broadly speaking, the darker the brew, the greater the heat. Brewer's malt does not change much in appearance during its conversion from barley, but the taste is very different. While a barley grain is tough and tasteless, malt is more brittle and recognizably "malty"

Cracking and milling

The brewer's first task on receiving a consignment of malt is to prepare it for the mashing process. At the brewery, the malt is cleaned, graded and weighed before the grains are cracked between pairs of steel rollers in the mill, which is often at the top of the building. A good miller will crack the husk and break the grain into fragments without making much flour, which is of no use to the brewer. Malt dust is highly inflammable and can harm the nose and throat if inhaled. Special precautions are taken in each part of the brewery where malt is handled.

Before mashing, any adjuncts to be used are mixed with the cracked malt. These are chosen from other, inferior grains, notably maize, rice and soft wheat unsuitable for baking, and help the brewer to hold down his costs.

Mashing

This mixture of malt and adjuncts is called the grist. It now enters the mash tun, where it is mixed with hot water for a period of about two hours. Mashing takes the process of transforming the starch and protein contained in the malt into soluble sugars one stage further. The agents of this activity are chemical compounds called enzymes, which act as catalysts for chemical reactions in all living cells. Enzymes are very sensitive to variations in temperature, so the heat of the mash tun must be very carefully controlled.

▼ The malting floor. The malt is turned over periodically to separate the grains and maintain an even temperature.

Lagers are brewed by the decoction mashing method, in which the grist and the liquor are mixed at 35-40°C (95-104°F) before being mashed at 65°C (149°F). Infusion mashing is employed for English-type beers and the temperature remains at approximately 65°C (149°F) throughout.

Instead of uncovered wooden mash tuns, modern breweries have large stainless steel or cast iron containers with lids to prevent steam and heat from escaping. The liquid resulting from the mashing process is called the wort. It is filtered out, leaving behind the spent solids of the grist. To extract the last of the wort, these are then sparged. This process involves spraying water from rotating metal arms attached to the inside of the mash tun.

Boiling in the copper

The wort must go through one more stage before it is ready to undergo fermentation and become beer. Hops and extra sugars are added and the mixture is boiled vigorously for up to two hours. In the process any remaining harmful bacteria are destroyed.

The boiling vessel is called the copper, though in recent years stainless steel containers have begun to replace the traditional coppers. They are far easier to clean, although copper is still more efficient at conducting heat from the furnace or steam to the wort itself.

The amount and variety of hops added in the copper differ according to the type of beer to be brewed. Sometimes all the hops are fed in at the start of boiling, but many brewers hold back a proportion until some minutes before the end of the process. Vigorous boiling is necessary to ensure that the maximum amounts of oils and resins are extracted from the hops.

Immediately boiling is completed, the wort must be cooled by attemperation to about 15°C (59°F), the right temperature for adding the yeast for fermentation.

▼ Adding hops to the wort in a large copper at the start of the boiling stage.

▼ Stream-lined coppers in a modern brewery.

How beer is brewed

The diagram shows the main stages of the brewing process which turn the basic raw materials (on the left) into finished beer and its by-products (on the right). Beer-making begins with the malting of the raw barley grains. The malted grains are cracked by the rollers in the mills to prepare them for mashing, where they are mixed with hot water. The spent solids that remain after mashing and sparging are sold off as cattle feed. The mashed wort is next boiled in the copper. Here the dried hops from the oast-house are added, as well as any special sugars that may be required for the particular variety of beer. After boiling, the wort is again drained off and the remaining waste matter may be used for fertilizer. Next, the yeast is taken out of cold store and added to the wort in the fermentation vessel. As the yeast multiplies in the wort, sugars are broken down into alcohol and carbon dioxide. After fermentation, the beer is placed in a settling vessel so that any impurities can separate out. Various forms of filtration may also be employed before the beer is sent to the storage tanks to await bottling, or is racked directly into metal or wooden barrels.

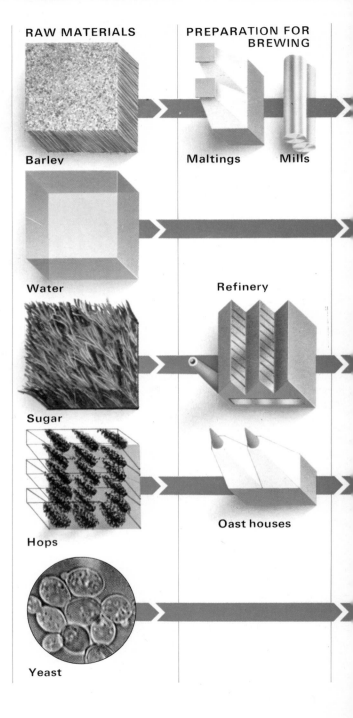

RAW MATERIALS

Barley

Water

Sugar

Hops

Yeast

PREPARATION FOR BREWING

Maltings

Mills

Refinery

Oast houses

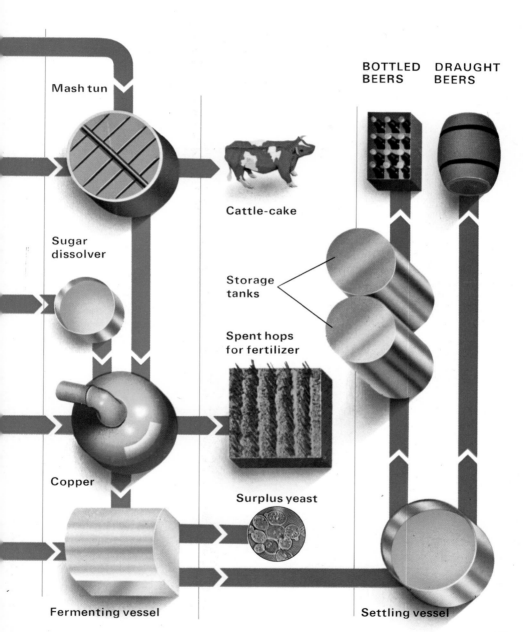

Mash tun

Cattle-cake

BOTTLED BEERS

DRAUGHT BEERS

Sugar dissolver

Storage tanks

Spent hops for fertilizer

Copper

Surplus yeast

Fermenting vessel

Settling vessel

Yeast and fermentation

Yeast cells are among the most active of living substances. In suitable conditions they reproduce and multiply constantly. Beer wort, rich in sugars, is an ideal environment for yeast, which converts the sugars into equal amounts of alcohol and carbon dioxide.

To halt the activity of the yeast until it is needed, the brewer keeps it in cold storage. When the wort is ready for fermentation, a small quantity of yeast is taken out and mixed with a little of the wort to make up a solution. The remaining wort is run into a large vat and the yeast solution is added.

There are two classes of yeast used by brewers, which produce different kinds of fermentation. In the top-fermentation process, used for British-type beers, a creamy head, up to a metre high, builds up after only a few hours. This is composed of carbon dioxide bubbles rising to the surface and bringing yeast cells with them. The surplus yeast is removed by "paddling" the head.

In the alternative, bottom-fermentation system, the yeast separates to the floor of the vat. This method is used in the brewing of lager-type beers.

Top-fermentation is complete within six days, while bottom-fermentation takes longer and the vat is kept much cooler. In Germany the fermentation period is between five and fourteen days at 5-10°C (41-50°F). In America, the wort spends six to nine days in the vat at a slightly higher temperature to start with which is reduced as fermentation proceeds.

Racking and storage

Once fermentation is complete, the beer must be cleared of spent yeast before being racked into casks or storage vats, or being sent to be bottled or canned. In the most automated breweries, a centrifuge is used to remove the yeast, while extra finings are added to clear any haziness in the brew.

Every effort is made to ensure that no contaminating matter remains in the beer after the elaborate precautions taken at every stage of the brewing process. To this end, most commercial beers are filtered and many are pasteurized. Among the most widely used filtering agents is *Kieselguhr*,

▶ Skimming or "paddling" the yeast head on a top-fermentation brew in the fermenting vessel. This removes spent yeast and other foreign matter.
The head is collected into tanks where it is treated for future use. After this head has been removed another one forms and helps protect the beer from contamination.

Coopering is the ancient craft of making watertight wooden barrels. For many centuries, the coopers were responsible not only for making beer casks, but for ensuring they were of the correct capacity. Oak is the best material for a cask, which will last for up to 30 years. The staves are cut to special shapes so that they can be forced into curved positions after heating. They are held in place by a series of iron hoops. The increasing cost of wood and the difficulty of cleaning wooden casks after prolonged use have led to their replacement by metal containers. Today, the art of the cooper is gradually dying out although wooden barrels are much in demand among home-brewers who prefer beer "from the wood"

which is derived from the fossilized skeletons of microscopic organisms.

Pasteurization is mainly used in the finishing of bottled beers and involves heating the full bottle or can to a high temperature for a very short period of time. This kills off any remaining bacteria in the beer. Chilling is also an important and widespread treatment for bottled beer. There is no doubt that pasteurization has an effect on the flavour of the brew, but opinion among beer-drinkers varies as to whether it improves it or not.

Bottling and canning plants are integral parts of modern breweries. They are often the most up-to-date in their technology, ensuring a continuous flow of bottles by conveyor belt. They move from the cleaning and sterilization unit to be filled under pressure by a machine which will handle up to 400 bottles a minute. They are then taken to the crown-corking machine where the metal caps are stamped into position. Pasteurization often takes place at this stage.

The most recent innovation in the storage of beer is the keg. Keg beer is a draught brew which is then treated in much the same way as bottled beer. It is sealed into large metal casks by a layer of carbon dioxide which prevents air from getting to the beer and adversely affecting it. Thus keg beer will keep for longer than the cask-conditioned traditional beer in its wooden barrel, though its treatment with carbon dioxide influences the final flavour.

From brewer to drinker

Many beers are often transported in large tanker lorries rather than in the casks themselves. The beer can then be piped into special tanks in the cellars of hotels, bars or pubs with a large beer consumption. Tankers are also used to transport beer from the brewery to the bottling plant.

The original method of delivery was,

▲ The traditional method of delivering beer from the brewery, now seen mainly at competitions and festivals.

of course, by horse-drawn dray. A lot of breweries still maintain a team of highly-trained shire horses, though only to take part in beer festivals and special competitions. In a few cases, however, recent increases in petrol prices have again made horse-drawn delivery an economic proposition for short journeys.

Once the beer has reached the retailer, there are various methods by which it can be served from the cask or keg. The simplest and oldest method was to set the cask at a height on a shelf, open the tap and let the beer flow out by gravity. But as alehouses became more careful about keeping beer and moved the casks to the cooler cellar, the constant running up and down to refill glasses became inefficient, not to say exhausting.

A system was therefore devised by which beer could be forced up from the cellar through a pipe attached to the barrel on the vacuum principle, by means of a handle at the bar. Later on, electric pumps were introduced which performed the same suction action but eliminated the physical effort. Apart from their nostalgic appeal, the only advantage possessed by hand-pumps over the electric variety is their ability to produce a smoother creamy head on the beer in the glass.

The advent of keg beers has introduced a further refinement in the dispensing of beer. Because they are already under pressure in the metal container, it is necessary only to have a mechanism to open a spout which allows the carbon dioxide surrounding the beer to force it upwards through the pipe. As a result, keg beers are more fizzy than the stiller cask-conditioned varieties prized by traditional beer enthusiasts.

Varieties of beer

1 Irish stout is brewed from a black malt and is popular all over the world.
2 Barley wine is closer in strength and body to a table wine than a beer.
3 Brown ale, a sweet-tasting top-fermented beer is specially brewed for bottling.
4 Bitter is the most popular of British top-fermented beers and several hundred varieties are available.
5 Light ale is a well carbonated bottled beer.
6 Draught lager is light in colour and sparkling in consistency.

Although the sequence of events in the making of beer is common to brewers all over the world, the variety of the end-product is almost infinite. With the traditionally brewed cask-conditioned beers, there can even be differences between one cask and the next made to the same recipe —usually a slight change in flavour due to variable fermentation conditions in the cask itself.

The type and quantity of the ingredients chosen, the temperature and the duration of the basic processes, all can be skilfully

blended by the brewer to produce a beer that is unique. Recent years have seen the expansion of brewing companies beyond national boundaries and attempts to standardize products by reproducing the recipes of Dublin or Copenhagen in Lagos or Kuala Lumpur. But, especially in Europe, there has been a counter movement back to local brews, based on the particular water or malt of each area.

The strength of beer

In terms of its effect on the drinker, perhaps the most obvious distinction between one beer and another is the alcoholic strength. This depends on the proportion of sugars to liquor in the brew, since it is the sugars which are converted into alcohol during the fermentation stage. The brewer can control the strength of his beer in various ways, including the addition of extra sugars before boiling in the copper and ensuring that a residue of malt sugar remains unfermented in the finished beer. The latter method also contributes to the fullness of body of the beer when it is ready for drinking.

The alcoholic strength of beer is measured in two distinct ways. In some countries, the method is similar to that used for wine or spirits whereby the percentage of alcohol by volume in the beer is calculated. The traditional method in Germany and Britain involves measuring the concentration of sugar in the unfermented wort, either in "degrees Plato" or in degrees of Original Gravity. The use of the hydrometer to work out the strength of the wort is described in detail on page 50, in the Activities section.

Beer and food

Like wine, beer is an ideal accompaniment for food, both with meals and in them. In Central Europe, the lagers of Germany and Czechoslovakia are widely associated with the characteristic sausages and sauerkraut of Bohemia and Bavaria, while beer straight from the metal can seems an appropriate partner for the convenience food "TV dinner".

Beer's main contribution to cookery is as a flavouring for meat dishes, particurly those involving beef. In Belgium, *Carbonnades Flamandes* (steak stewed in beer) is a national dish. But beer is equally useful in sweet recipes, and in earlier times most puddings would include it as an ingredient. Danish beer and bread soup, eaten at breakfast, also dates from medieval times.

MOCK AND HERBAL BEERS
Herbal beers are those in which a flavouring other than hops is used. Before hops were established as the universal additive to the wort, many different herbs, flowers and fruits were part of the brewer's stock of ingredients, including cowslips, elderberries and blackberries. In the present century, home brewing in rural Norway involved the addition of bog myrtle to the wort. The only widespread herbal flavouring in use today is spruce, which is mixed with the hops, in concentrated oil form, by some Scandinavian brewers.

Drinks which resemble beer but have little or no alcoholic content are known as mock beers. Sarsaparilla, an American drink, has a taste like liquorice or treacle, while ginger beer, when brewed from stone ginger which is yeasted, has a minimal alcohol content.

Beer in society

Nowadays, beer-drinking is for most people strictly a leisure time activity. But until other drinks like tea and coffee became widely enough available and cheap enough, beer was the everyday beverage of the mass of the population. Unlike tea or coffee, though, beer was an intoxicant and its association with drunkenness, disorder and pleasure has made it a subject of controversy down the centuries.

During medieval times, there were occasional pronouncements on the evils of drink from bishops and other religious leaders, but it was not until the rise of Protestantism in Northern Europe that the first concerted attacks on the consumption of alcohol were mounted. The lavish festivities of the Middle Ages were regarded as wasteful and ungodly, while the new virtues were those of thrift and hard work, to which large-scale beer-drinking was clearly not conducive. Additionally, taverns and ale-houses were the haunts of anti-social characters, be they highwaymen and beggars or the politically discontented.

Swords and salvation

The contrast between approbation and condemnation of beer has continued into modern times. Beer remained a focus of ceremony and ritual, most notably in the Prussian student societies of pre-Nazi Germany. Membership of one of these groups, whose main activities were drinking and duelling, was obligatory for anyone wishing to join the political or military establishment. Duelling scars were a matter

▼ Members of Prussian student societies in the pre- 1914 era were expected to be equally adept at drinking and duelling.

▼ A meeting of the Salvation Army, founded in London to combat poverty and alcoholism in the slums of the 19th century.

▲ Police breaking open casks of illicit alcohol during the Prohibition era in the United States.

A victory for temperance

The temperance movement had some successes. In most places it was able to influence decisions to restrict the sale of alcoholic drinks to young people and to limit the hours in which beer could be bought. Its most important victory was in the United States where, in 1919, the Volstead Act prohibited altogether the manufacture and sale of any drink with an alcohol content of over 0·5 per cent (most of today's beers contain at least 4 per cent alcohol).

The immediate result was not a rise in sobriety and morality, as the reformers had intended, but precisely the opposite. There was a spectacular growth in organized crime, made possible by the fact that many normally law-abiding people were willing

of pride, while the members had also to be able to down *Stein* after *Stein* of strong lager without forgetting the many toasts and drinking songs which accompanied them.

On the other side of the fence, strong temperance movements grew up as industrialization proceeded in the 19th century. Many of these reformers, like General Booth, founder of the Salvation Army, had social as well as religious motives. They were particularly concerned about the connection of drunkenness with the poverty and hopelessness of slum-dwellers in the new industrial cities of Northern Europe.

Often, though, the cause of alcoholism was not beer but cheap spirits. In some cases, the effect of beer was contrasted favourably with that of more potent beverages. In a famous pair of engravings by the English caricaturist Hogarth, ''Gin Lane'' shows scenes of destitution and degradation while ''Beer Lane'' is full of contentment and prosperity.

> **ALE FOR HEALTH**
> The history of the medicinal uses of beer dates back to Biblical times when Egyptian physicians, like some doctors today, regarded beer as a tonic. Saxon tribes mixed ale with certain herbs to treat various ailments, while a mixture of beer, holy water and garlic was said to ward off evil spirits.
>
> Similar herb and beer mixtures continued to be prescribed up to the 18th century, including a senna pod ale, sold in taverns as a remedy for digestive complaints. Today, the Czech lager, *Plzensky Prazdroj,* has medical approval as a treatment for ulcers because of its alkalizing effect on the stomach, while certain bottled beers act as mild stimulants for patients recuperating from long illnesses.

to pay black market prices rather than abstain from alcohol. Gangsters like Al Capone moved in to organize illegal supplies of bootleg liquor, much of which was substandard or even lethal. In 1933, the authorities admitted defeat and the Act was repealed. Today, the main centres of absolute prohibition are in Asia and Africa. The strength of organized religion has made certain Indian states "dry", and the strictures against alcohol in the Koran forbid alcohol in Arab countries.

▼ The *Oktoberfest*, held annually in Munich, is a celebration of the quality and variety of Bavarian beers.

Taxes and festivals

The two opposing attitudes towards beer persist in present-day society, though disapproval takes the milder, if painful, form of taxation. In most countries, alcoholic drinks are one of the first targets of governments needing to raise greater revenue. The cheapness and the popularity of home brewing is due mostly to the fact that a large percentage of the price paid for a glass of beer in a bar goes directly in taxation to the government.

Despite the great social changes of the past two centuries, echoes of the great medieval celebrations linger on in events

like the Munich *Oktoberfest*, where many thousands of litres of beer are consumed in a carnival atmosphere. There are faint echoes, too, of the elaborate formal toasts of medieval feasts in the terms ordinary drinkers use to compliment each other, such as the Scandinavian "skol" or the English "cheers".

National tastes

Far more than with wine, beers and beer-drinking habits vary widely from country to country. In this they resemble the differences in cuisine between nations, who may use similar ingredients but produce very different kinds of food from them.

Dark, top-fermented beers are popular only in Britain and Germany today, while the rest of the world produces lighter, bottom-fermented beers. The differences between the two types extend to the ideal temperature at which each is drunk. The lager-type beers ferment at lower temperatures and are intended to be consumed chilled to bring out the flavour. The opposite holds true for British-style bitters and pale ales, which should be served at about 12-13°C (53-55°F) for their flavour to be fully apparent. These distinctions often confuse partisans of one type of beer, who find the other either frozen and tasteless or tepid and unsatisfying.

Similarly, customs concerned with mixing beer with other drinks vary from place to place. It is sometimes said that to mix the grape and the grain will inevitably lead to disaster, yet in Denmark, for instance, wine, beer and schnaps are frequently consumed in conjunction with each other. In Britain, where lager beers have only recently become popular, the drink is sometimes served with a dash of lime juice added. A more unusual mixture has been reported from Nigeria, where lager beer has been drunk with Coca-Cola.

Beer—the world drink

Among the fruits of European civilization taken by the colonizers and traders all over the world was beer. The most famous breweries in the United States, including Pabst and Schlitz, were founded by immigrants. As well as importing large quantities from home, the Dutch, British and Germans began brewing in their foreign territories. As a result, the European beers gradually supplanted traditional alcoholic beverages in large parts of Africa and Asia.

The 20th century has brought a new element to the internationalization of beer. The growth in foreign travel and tourism has introduced many people to the drinking customs of other countries. As a result, it is now possible to find Danish lager or Irish stout, in draught or bottled form, in most capitals of the world.

Among the most recent converts to beer are the Japanese and the Arabs. Japan's brewing industry is among the fastest-growing in the world and it may be that, as in many other things, the skill and energy of Japanese brewers may eventually outstrip that of the West. Perhaps the day is not far off when Japanese brews are as

▲ The traditional way to drink home-brewed ale in West Africa is from a calabash. The region also has several well-equipped commercial breweries.

highly-prized as those of Germany and Czechoslovakia are today. The interest of the Arab nations in beer has not been daunted by the fact that their religion forbids alcohol. Some of them have begun to import from England large quantities of a non-alcoholic beer that tastes the same as the real thing.

The growing international trade in beers of many countries may help to offset the tendency towards standardization in modern commercial brewing techniques, as does the increasingly popular craft of home-brewing, which is described in the next section of this book.

Equipment for brewing

Brewing beer at home is a pastime that can now be enjoyed by all. For not only will most of the equipment necessary be found already in the house, thereby minimizing the original outlay, but the method of brewing can be varied to suit the individual.

You can choose either to mash malted barley to produce the fermentable sugars, or start with malt extract. The equipment needed will depend on which process you decide to adopt. However, the initial outlay need not be much and will soon be recuperated by producing beer at a fraction of the cost of commercial beers.

Recipes and equipment are for making five gallons of beer.

1 Dustbin
2 Electric boiler
3 Insulated food container
4 Boiling pan
5 Fermentation bin
6 Bottles
7 Siphon tube
8 Spoon
9 Cracked malt
10 Sugar
11 Yeast
12 Dried hops
13 Electric blender

Mashing

If you are going to brew your beer from grains, the first piece of equipment you will require will be a large container suitable for mashing (see p. 33). This needs to have a tap for draining the mash wort (the mixture of water and grains), and to be able to hold the quantity of liquor (the brewing term for water) at the required temperature. A five gallon electric boiler is ideal for this. These have the advantage that the liquid can be heated up to, and maintained at, the required temperature in the boiler itself.

Instead of the electric heater you can use a polythene bin with a tap and tight-fitting lid. With this method a 50 watt immersion heater, preferably with thermostat, can be used to raise the water to the required temperature. Alternatively, the water can be added preheated.

Either type of container will need to be well insulated in order to maintain the temperature of the wort.

This can be achieved by tightly wrapping the container in blankets or by placing it in a heat bath (see p.47). Maintaining the temperature in the "bath" by adding additional hot water as required, ensures that the correct temperature is kept within the mash tun.

A third alternative is a campers' four gallon insulated food container, again with tap. This makes an excellent mash tun well able to sustain the temperature for the required period of time. It can however be rather difficult to find at the required size. Which ever container you use, you will need a muslin bag or bucket with 3mm holes drilled in the base to hold the barley within the main container.

Boiling

The larger the boiler is, the more convenient it will be for boiling the wort with the hops and sugar. Again the electric boiler (5-10 gallon capacity) is an ideal piece of equipment, but do ensure that it is not used for any

other purpose to avoid the risk of contamination and off-flavours.

Also suitable is a 3-5 gallon capacity boiling pan or a "dixie", both of which can be heated on the stove. A large one gallon saucepan can be used but, the smaller the container, the more boiling sessions will be needed.

Fermentation

For primary fermentation, a large open vessel is required so that the yeast head can be skimmed and patted and the brew stirred with ease. You can therefore use an oak cask or large open earthenware jar. Many enthusiasts maintain that beer, especially bitter, will always taste better if fermented in wood. It must however be remembered that, being porous, wood will require much time and effort on the part of the brewer to prevent contamination occurring. When not in use, the wood must also not be allowed to dry out and contract. Earthenware jars are easier to clean but will normally prove excessively heavy for the job.

The most useful container is a plastic dustbin or a special brewing bin to hold five gallons of fermenting beer. These are cheap, light and easy to clean and have the advantage that they can be left empty for long periods, only needing a normal cleaning when next used. For ease of measurement the bin can be calibrated on the outside with gallon and half-gallon marks. During

the secondary fermentation, you will need an air-tight container which can be fitted with an airlock. A brewing bin with the airlock fitted into the lid can be used or, alternatively, a five gallon glass carboy. The carboy has the advantage that the liquid is visible. The beer might be clear at the top, and appear ready for racking, yet still contain settling yeast towards the bottom.

One or two gallon glass jars with ear handles are also ideal for secondary fermentation and are normally easy to acquire either from chemists or home brew suppliers.

An extra piece of equipment, which will quickly pay for itself in time and effort

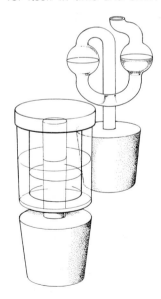

▲ Two common types of airlock used during fermentation.

▲ Sieve used for filtering the wort after mashing and boiling.

saved is a 5-7 gallon plastic bin with tap. This will prove useful as a general purpose container and also makes an excellent sparger when you require a large quantity of water to be sprayed over the mashed grains.

MINOR PIECES OF EQUIPMENT

Apart from the main pieces of equipment already mentioned, there are certain extra items which you will need before commencing your first brew. For removing the beer from the yeast sediment, you will need a 1-2m. length of siphon tubing — rubber can be used although clear plastic is preferable as it enables the siphoned liquid to be seen. When siphoning, there is a risk of some of the sediment being sucked up into the tube once you get near the bottom of the vessel. This is because, with the tube point-

▲ Large plastic watering can with rose attachment for sparging.

Care must be taken that the grains are not over crushed resulting in excessive powder which will affect the finished beer. If you do not have an extractor and are only dealing in small quantities of grain, you can crack grain by pressing it with a rolling pin or wine bottle.

If you are using a brewers' bin with tap when sparging the mash wort, it is easy to achieve a steady, even flow of liquor by using a rose from a watering can attached to a short length of tubing, in turn attached to the tap. Alternatively a 2-3 gallon watering-can does the job adequately, although it will require refilling half way through the sparging. A sieve will be needed for straining the wort as it drains out after the mashing has been completed. Alternatively a sheet of muslin inside a colander is just as effective.

During the secondary fermentation, air has to be excluded from the beer by using air-locks pushed into corks or preferably rubber bungs.

A thermometer and a

▲ Funnel for general use, e.g. priming the bottles. Can act as a filter with a disc attachment.

hydrometer are two essential tools which help the brewer to avoid errors occurring and to ensure that the brewing is proceeding according to plan. The use of the hydrometer is explained in detail later in the book (see p.50).

The only other item of equipment left for the brewer to find is the means of storing the beer before it is to be drunk, be it in barrels or bottles, and these are dealt with later. (See p.62.)

At various times during brewing, it is necessary to move large quantities of liquid, e.g. when the cooled wort is placed in the primary fermentation vessel and taken to a convenient place for fermentation to occur. As five gallons of liquid is a fairly heavy quantity to carry, it is a good idea to construct a simple trolley which will enable a bulk of liquid to be moved with comparative ease. A 40×40cm square of plywood or planking, with a castor fixed under each corner, can be cheaply and simply constructed.

ing downwards, the beer is being siphoned out in an upwards motion. The best way to avoid this happening is to buy a U-bend siphon tube which costs only a few pence. This you add on to the end of the flexible tubing, with the result that the beer is sucked downwards into the tube, so leaving the yeast sediment undisturbed.

At the preparing stage, you will need a long-handled wooden spoon and a plastic funnel. A calibrated one pint measuring jug and a quart jug will also prove useful additions when handling large quantities.

If you are brewing beer from malted grain, you will need to crack the grains before mashing to enable extraction to take place. Commercial breweries use roller presses which produce an evenly cracked grist. Unfortunately there does not yet seem to be any direct equivalent available for the home-brewer. The most suitable compromise is an electric blender which cracks the grain easily and quickly.

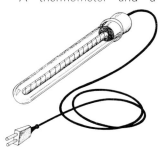

▲ Immersion heater with thermostat.

Brewing step-by-step

1 Cleaning and sterilizing

First ensure that there is no risk of the beer being wasted through contamination. Every item of equipment must be thoroughly cleaned and sterilized before use.

2 Cracking the malt

Before mashing, the malt must be prepared by being lightly crushed. This breaks the husk of the grain, so allowing the sugars to be extracted during the next stage.

5 Boiling

Hops and any extra sugar to be used are now added to the wort. This is boiled for 1-1½ hours to extract the flavouring and preserving qualities of the hops.

6 Pitching

After boiling, the wort is drained into the fermentation bin and cooled to 16-19°C (60-65°F). Next the yeast is pitched, or poured in, and the wort aerated by stirring.

3 Mashing

Cracked malt is added to hot water to give an overall temperature of 66-69°C (150-155°F). This is maintained for 1½-2 hours by insulation to convert and extract the fermentable sugars.

4 Sparging

The mixture of sugars and water, known as the wort, is now drained off the spent grains. Sparging, or spraying the grains, ensures all the sugars are removed.

7 Fermentation

Keep temperature at 16-19°C (60-65°F) and cover the bin until the head forms. Skim the head daily. After fermentation abates (4 days) siphon into gallon jars and fit air-locks.

8 Racking and storing

When fermentation has ceased and the beer has cleared, it is ready to be racked into bottles or casks for storage. Leave on average 3-4 weeks before drinking.

Cleaning and sterilizing

One of the problems that we are faced with in home-brewing is that bacteria are attracted to beer almost as much as we humans are. Airborne bacteria, especially wild yeast, is bound to contaminate a brew and the equipment sooner or later unless you adopt a plan of regularly cleaning equipment before and after use.

As this part of brewing is not normally the most popular, it is worth remembering when choosing your equipment, that plastic and glass are much easier to clean than some other materials.

▼ Protect brews from contamination by thoroughly cleaning all equipment used with hot water. Afterwards, sterilize with sulphur dioxide solution or Campden tablets. Avoid the use of detergents.

Cleaning and sterilizing

As is commonly known, pure alcohol is an effective agent against infection. However, beer is at risk of contamination at all the stages of its production, especially as it is a relatively weak alcoholic drink and one with low acid content — another natural line of defence. Hops, which are primarily added for enhancing the flavour, provide a certain preservative quality, but beer is mainly protected by the preventative treatment applied by the brewer.

Infection occurs either by airborne bacteria attacking the beer directly, or by the beer coming into contact at some point with an infected container or utensil. Direct airborne infection is most likely to occur either when the boiled wort is cooling or during the secondary fermentation after the protective yeast head has dropped. With the former, the boiler should be kept closely covered and in the latter case, an air-lock is used to prevent air reaching the beer.

Kitchen hygiene

In dealing with the equipment, the normal standards of hygiene that are applied in the kitchen must be followed. Household detergents, however, need to be avoided as does any form of grease, as the smallest deposit left in a vessel can destroy the head on the finished beer. This should be remembered when cleaning beer glasses and mugs. Without washing-up liquids, hot water and a scouring pad do the job quite easily—especially if the cleaning is done immediately after use before any deposit has dried out.

Use a nylon wool scouring pad if available. They are easier to sterilize by boiling in water than the sponge pad-type. Avoid wirewool which scratches surfaces and increases the risk of contamination eventually occurring.

Household bleach

There are certain commercially prepared chlorine-based agents on the market which can be found in your local brewing shop, but it is cheaper and just as easy to prepare your own.

The most convenient source of chlorine is found in ordinary household bleach. Made up to a 10 per cent solution by adding one part of bleach to nine parts water, this will deal with heavily contaminated articles such as any second hand bottles you may acquire.

First, wash the item to remove surface dirt in the normal way and drain. Then wash thoroughly with the bleach solution and allow to stand for a couple of minutes before rinsing. Any item that has been treated with bleach must be thoroughly rinsed to remove any trace of the characteristic chlorine smell.

Chlorine can be used at any strength but the 10 per cent solution should kill any wild yeast or bacteria. Avoid getting neat bleach on the skin and do not use one which has a strong scent, such as pine.

Sodium dioxide

For normal equipment, sulphur dioxide is the most popular sterilizing agent used. This is produced in solution by adding sodium metabisulphite to water in a 10 per cent solution. Dissolve two ounces of the white powder in warm water, to make a total volume of one pint. Alternatively, Campden tablets which contain 60 per cent sulphur dioxide in solution can be used. Crush the tablets between two teaspoons and stir in well to hot water to dissolve.

An additional attribute of sulphur dioxide is that, in contact with bleach, the two become chemically inactive.

Therefore, after a piece of equipment has been cleaned with bleach, any traces of chlorine can be neutralized by washing with a 10 per cent solution of sodium metabisulphite before the final rinse. (However do not use the same treatment the other way around.)

A stock solution of sodium metabisulphite can be made up for general sterilization by diluting two fluid ounces of the 10 per cent mixture with a further pint of water. This can then be used for the treatment of bins, bottles and small items etc. Afterwards, the stock solution should be discarded and a fresh mixture used for each session.

During use, the efficiency of the solution can be checked by adding a pinch of citric acid. This will produce a spontaneous discharge of sulphur gas if still active. After cleaning the items as directed with hot water and

▼ Common type of bottle brush available in different sizes.

▲ Twist type of brush, more effective but also more expensive.

scouring pad, wash well with the solution and rinse with cold water.

Narrow-necked containers such as bottles and demijohns can be cleaned with a bottle brush. Afterwards a few drops of solution in the bottom of each will keep your containers fresh during storage. To avoid making up fresh sterilizing solution each time you can store a stock solution in a container such as a thoroughly cleansed washing-up liquid bottle or a large fruit juice jar.

Ingredients: the malt

Brewing beer in your own home has now become sufficiently popular for home brew kits to appear on the market. These may vary substantially in quality but are all simplicity itself to follow, requiring a minimum of equipment, time and expertise. On the part of the brewer the drawback of course is that they are not necessarily the cheapest way to produce beer and they can only produce a version of the beer. A quick glance at the recipe section indicates the sort of variety that can be found with each type of beer.

In the following pages the summary of ingredients given will indicate how one can achieve such variety in brewing.

▼ Malt extract is available in liquid or powder form.

Malt is the basis for all beer, supplying the main bulk of the fermentable sugars in any brew. It comes in the following forms:
1. Malted barley grain (malt).
2. Malt extract.
3. Malt adjuncts.

If malted barley grain, commonly abbreviated to malt, is to be used as opposed to malt extract, then it will need to be mashed in order to extract the starch content and convert it to fermentable sugar (see p.47). The extra work involved is amply repaid by the added control over quality and flavour.

If you buy malt from a reputable home-brewing shop, there is little need to worry about quality, but as there is no information supplied with the grain at sale concerning its extraction rate, nitrogen level or age, it is as well to know a few points about its appearance which will be an indication of its standard.

A sample of the grains should contain little dust or foreign matter. They should be of even size and plump in shape. The grain should easily crush between thumbnail and forefinger and the inside should taste fairly sweet. The inside should also be quite floury indicating a low nitrogen level and with no large air pocket caused by kilning too rapidly. The nitrogen content,

Some malts and adjuncts
1 Crystal malt
2 Pale malt
3 Roast barley
4 Flaked barley
5 Flaked maize
6 Brumore wheat flour

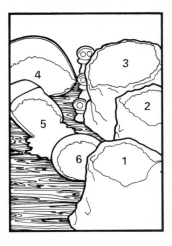

▲ A 19th century maltings.

although very low, is important in the brewing process as too high a nitrogen level can throw a haze in the finished beer which is very difficult to remove. Too low a content can affect the fermentation.

Pale malt is the basis of all grain beers, i.e. beers brewed from malted barley as opposed to malt extract, as it produces the highest rate of fermentable sugars, producing a gravity of up to 1030 at 1 lb to the gallon.

Pale malt is therefore used as the main ingredient in grain beers and darker malts are added to alter the final colour and flavour.

Lager malt has the lowest kilning temperature during malting and is consequently very light in colour. Prior to kilning, the short germination period employed produces high enzymatic activity. It is similar in strength to pale malt.

Crystal or caramel malt has already had its starch content converted to sugar. If you taste a grain of crystal malt it will be noticeably sweeter than a grain of pale malt. It is kilned at a slightly higher temperature than pale malt and has a more golden colour.

Roast barley As the name implies roast barley is an unmalted barley grain, roast-ed to a dark reddish-brown colour and recommended for brown ale and dry stouts. As with black malt, the sugar content is so low that roasted barley is not really affected by not being malted.

Black malt is roasted at high temperatures of about 230°C (450°F) to caramelize the sugar, giving it both a rich flavour and colour. As with roast barley, black malt does not contribute any significant quality of sugar and is used to add flavouring and colouring to a beer. It is used in stouts.

Malt extract
There are different grades of malt extract on the market,

some of which, such as the extract flavoured with cod-liver oil, are unsuitable for our purposes. However, the brewing of beer is so popular nowadays that you should experience no difficulty in finding a suitable supply. Malt extract is sold either as a syrup or as a dry powder and with both, the advantage is in the fact that they require no mashing as the sugars have already been converted. Beers made entirely from extract are not particularly recommended as they tend to produce a somewhat nutty-flavoured beer and cannot reproduce the quality of a true grain beer. However, excellent beers can be produced by combining the two, using the extract in place of pale malt. Although mashing will be required for some of the grains used, it is a simpler process requiring less time and equipment. The recipe section covers both grain beers and the extract and grain brews.

MALT ADJUNCTS

Some people decry the use of any adjunct, claiming some commercial brewers add them to lower costs at the expense of quality. For home-brewing this is not the case and, treated with care, small quantities can improve flavour and be an aid to the brewing process.

Flaked maize Probably the most used of adjuncts, flaked maize contributes a pleasant flavour to lagers and bitters. It can also help to

prevent a haze in finished beer.

Flaked rice has the advantages of maize but does not contribute any flavour in the small quantities used.

Flaked barley produces a pleasant grainy flavour to the beer. However, it does involve a haze risk so is best kept for stouts where it also helps head retention.

Torrified barley Being larger than the normal grain, torrified barley helps to produce an efficient mash by allowing the wort to drain more readily during sparging. Use approximately $1\text{-}1\frac{1}{2}$ oz per gallon.

Wheat malt has a high nitrogen content compared to barley malt and so should be used sparingly (1-2 oz per gallon). Added to the bulk of the grain for mashing, it does however produce a pleasant grainy flavour and is suited to stouts.

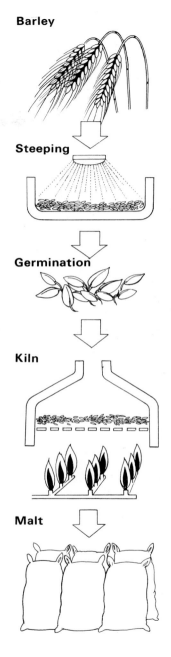

Barley

Steeping

Germination

Kiln

Malt

▶ Steeping initiates the growth process.
Germination under strict temperature control converts the barley to malt. Kilning terminates growth and dries the malt for storage.

Other ingredients

The other main constituents of beer are hops, yeast and sugar. As with malt, there are many variations with each type of ingredient and those most commonly used are listed in the following pages.

Although it is far too impractical to keep all the ingredients mentioned in stock, experimenting with them will gradually show you which are most suited to your requirements.

▲ Hops on the bine.

HOPS

Hops are principally used in the brewing of beer to lengthen its life and add flavour.

Not so long ago, the only hops available to the home-brewer were often an unspecified variety of unknown origin and quality. Nowadays however, we benefit from the renewed popularity of the brewing craft in having a fair selection of hops available. The hopping rate varies from one type of hop to another but average use is $\frac{2}{3}$ oz per gallon of beer. The more hops used, the more bitter the beer.

Other than the natural dried flower, hops can be bought either as hop concentrate or hop oil. These are not normally recommended for home-brewing, although the use of hop oil for dry hopping (see p.53), does obviate the need for keeping odd amounts of hops over from a brew. If you have access to a hop merchant who will supply you with hops, you will find it substantially cheaper than dealing with a home-brew shop. You will however need the means of carefully storing the larger quantities that you will have to buy. Hops should be stored in air-tight containers shaded from daylight and heat, to prevent deterioration.

The main constituents in the hop flower which play a part in beer-making are the soft resins, oils and tannin.

Soft resins

These are made up of alpha acid (Humulon) and beta acid (Lupulon).

By percentage weight of the hop cone, there is a higher beta than alpha acid content. However, although both supply bittering and preserving qualities to the beer, alpha acid supplies the major share. Hops are quoted in terms of their alpha acid content.

Oils

The essential oils produce the distinctive aroma of the hops. Unfortunately most of the oils evaporate from the wort during the boiling period. This can best be offset by dry hopping towards the end of secondary fermentation.

Tannin

Tannin is an important constituent of the hop because of its ability to precipitate protein matter out of the wort. If allowed to remain, the protein would tend to form a haze in the finished beer.

The tannin content is found on the petals and stems of the cone and its efficiency is improved by a violent boiling action whereby the cones "roll" through the wort as opposed to floating on the surface.

Mature hops should be light green in colour with a certain amount of spring

▶ This method of attaching strings to a line for the growing hops to climb up has now virtually died out.

▲ The home-brewer can buy selected hops ready dried for immediate use.

indicating freshness. Rubbing a sample between the hands releases the oils which should have a pleasant mild aroma. Too little or too harsh a flavour indicates poor hops.

MAIN TYPES OF HOPS
Goldings is an excellent hop, light in colour and slightly smaller than the other varieties. Its delicate flavour makes it ideal for dry hopping. Used in bitters, light and pale ales.

Fuggles Along with Goldings, Fuggles accounts for the majority of hops used in brewing. It is stronger flav- oured and has larger cones than Goldings. Fuggles is principally used by the home- brewer for darker beers such as stouts and brown ales.

Hallertau is an excellent German hop with a firm, dark green seedless cone. Normally used with lagers, it is also a pleasant addition when used with Goldings in bitters and pale ales.

Saaz is a seedless hop which produces a delicate dry flavour. Unfortunately it is difficult for home-brewers to get hold of, but certainly worth the effort for lagers.

Northern Brewer Looks are deceptive with this hop as its colour and state give it the appearance of being a poor hop. Strongly flavoured with a high acid content, it enables the hopping rate to be lowered on some brews. Excellent with stouts.

Bullion has a strong and distinctively bitter aroma and should always be used in conjunction with another hop. As a guide, use one part Bullion to three parts other hops. It is a pleasant addition in stouts and bitters.

Bramling Cross is a variety of Goldings which is par- ticularly easy to grow and has a high disease resist- ance. If available, this hop is worth using with bitters, pale and light ales.

Progress hops have a fine aroma and flavour and are best used with Goldings.

YEAST
Yeast is a single-celled bac- terium which, when fed with a sugary solution, is able to multiply at a remarkable rate producing equal quan- tities of alcohol and carbon dioxide.

Bakers' yeast is not suit- able for brewing. It leaves a bad flavour in the beer and does not settle at all well, making it wasteful when syphoning.

Wine yeast should not be employed either, being only suited to conditions present in a wine must.

The two strains of yeast used are the top fermenting brewers' yeast and the bot- tom fermenting lager yeasts.

► A yeast solution is pitched into a tank to start fermentation in a commercial brew.

Top fermenting yeasts should only be used with beers as they are not suitable for lagers. They produce a thick frothy head which protects the fermenting beer during the primary fermentation. They also work at slightly higher temperatures than most lager yeasts, so allowing a shorter fermentation period. The yeast head, if left, will eventually sink to the bottom with the risk of imparting a yeast-bitten flavour to the beer as it settles. To avoid this, the head is periodically skimmed. (See p.58.)

Bottom fermenting yeasts prefer to work at lower temperatures and produce a slower fermentation. A yeast crop is formed, but less than with a top fermenter, and as this cannot be relied upon to protect the brew, fermentation is carried out in a closed container. As closed fermentation throughout cuts the risk of airborne infection and as lager yeasts produce such a firm sediment, bottom fermenting yeasts are becoming increasingly popular for use with beers as well as with lagers.

There are nowadays several strains of yeast marketed, either in tablet or granulated form. The packet states that the contents are sufficient for a certain size brew, normally 5 gallons. However don't worry if you have a packet for 4 gallons and you are brewing, for instance, 5 gallons. In theory the brew could be started with a single cell.

Always be prepared to experiment with different types of yeast as some will perform more satisfactorily than others. Generally the quality of the yeast can be judged by its ability to form and maintain a yeast head during primary fermentation.

Apart from buying packeted yeast from a home-brew shop, you can start a brew with the yeast sediment from one of your own bottles or from a commercial bottled beer which has been naturally conditioned, such as Guinness. Three days before you commence fermentation, stand the bottle for 24 hours to settle. Then carefully empty the contents leaving the last 2cm behind. Add one dessertspoon of malt extract and one of sugar mixed with $\frac{1}{4}$ pint of hot water. When cooled, add two pinches of citric acid, insert the airlock and leave until required.

SUGARS

Sugar is a beneficial ingredient in a brew as it helps the beer to mature more quickly and, in higher gravity beers, keeps the haze-forming nitrogen level down. The over-use of sugar is not wise as it produces a thin drink for the gravity given. By weight, it is advisable for the sugar not to exceed one third of the fermentable ingredients. Whenever adding sugar, dissolve thoroughly by stirring.

▼ Types of sugar the home-brewer can use

1 Coarse brown sugar
2 Glucose chips
3 Granulated white sugar
4 Molasses
5 Soft brown sugar
6 Golden syrup
7 Invert sugar
8 Light brown sugar

White Sugar

White sugar (sucrose) is the most commonly used sugar in home-brewing. Produced from sugar cane or beet, it is sold as granulated, cube, icing or caster sugar. However, the home-brewer is mainly interested in the cheapest version, which is granulated. Chemically they are all identical, but white sugar, apart from being the cheapest brewing sugar, also has the highest extraction rate.

Invert Sugar

This is of great advantage to the brewer as it is immediately fermentable by yeast, so reducing the risk of a brew becoming contaminated before the protective head has been formed. Invert sugar can be bought at home-brew shops but, due to its crystalline water con-

tent, the quantity required has to be adjusted by an additional 25 per cent, ($2\frac{1}{2}$ lb invert sugar to 2 lb household white).

However, household sugar can be simply inverted during the brewing process by using the normal quantity plus 2 teaspoons of citric acid added to the wort for boiling with the hops. The boiling action and the acid content naturally inverts the sugar. Afterwards, add 2 teaspoons of sodium bicarbonate or calcium carbonate to neutralize the acidity.

Demerara, Barbados etc.

These brown sugars, although more expensive than white, do impart flavour as well as colour. They are mainly added to stouts and brown ales. However, the moisture content does lower

extraction rate slightly.

◄ In the past, most breweries had their own water supply from river or well. Nowadays however they use public supplies which they treat to their requirements. Treatment of tap water is also necessary for best results with home brewing.

Glucose chips A cheap method of adding sugar, although the large chips take some time to dissolve. Adds slight colour and a dry flavour to the beer.

Lactose The most common of the non-fermentable sugars, lactose is used to sweeten stouts. (See stout recipes.)

Caramel is readily available as liquid gravy browning and is used as a colourant to darken beers but has little flavour.

WATER

The quality of water — or liquor as the breweries call it — plays an important role in the finished beer.

Some regions have grown famous for beers brewed with local water — such as Dublin stout and Burton bitter. As we are restricted to the water of a particular area, it is necessary for us to adjust the water as required. The basic aim of water treatment is to alter the acidity of the wort to suit the type of beer that is being brewed.

Hard water suits pale ale, light ale and bitters, so if you live in a soft water area, these beers will benefit from Epsom salts (magnesium sulphate) and Gypsum (calcium sulphate).

Water for milds, brown ales and stouts needs to be fairly soft, so hard water needs to be treated with common salt (sodium chloride) and sodium carbonate. Water for lager is best treated with salt and citric acid.

The amount of additive will naturally vary with the degree of hardness or softness in the water. A fair average in all cases is half a teaspoon per gallon added before mashing. Amounts can then be varied if necessary in the light of experience. There are also brands of water treatments now on the market which work consistently well.

	Water required	Treatment per gallon added before mashing
Bitter	Hard	$\frac{1}{2}$ tsp Gypsum; $\frac{1}{4}$ tsp Epsom salts
Light	Hard	$\frac{1}{2}$ tsp Gypsum; $\frac{1}{4}$ tsp Epsom salts
Pale	Hard	$\frac{1}{2}$ tsp Gypsum; $\frac{1}{4}$ tsp Epsom salts
Lager	Soft	Boil the water for 30 mins $\frac{1}{2}$ tsp common salt; $\frac{1}{2}$ tsp citric acid
Stout	Soft	$\frac{1}{2}$ tsp common salt
Mild	Soft	$\frac{1}{2}$ tsp salt; $\frac{1}{2}$ tsp calcium carbonate
Brown	Soft	$\frac{1}{2}$ tsp salt; $\frac{1}{2}$ tsp calcium carbonate

Brewing methods

Now that the range of ingredients used in the various types of beers has been introduced, we can go on to the most important part of brewing — namely the method of converting these same ingredients into a pleasant end-product.

As already mentioned, beer can either be made from grain, malt extract or a mixture of the two.

Below are two simple recipes for bitter. The procedure for each is initially different as is explained in the directions that follow.

Recipe A
5 lb pale malt
8 oz crystal malt
1 lb white sugar
3 oz Goldings hops
Top fermenting beer yeast

Recipe B
4 lb malt extract
8 oz crystal malt
1 lb white sugar
3 oz Goldings hops
Top fermenting beer yeast

To obtain a true quality beer, it is necessary to use an "all grains" recipe such as recipe A. But if you wish to follow the simpler procedure of a no-mash or limited mash brew, then a recipe such as B would be followed.

The reason that different methods are used is that some grain adjuncts do not require to be mashed because either the starch content has already been converted to sugar, or the low amount involved does not warrant extraction.

Mashing required
Pale malt
Flaked maize
Flaked rice
Flaked barley
Wheat flour

Mashing not required
Malt extract
Crystal malt
Black malt
Roast barley and malt
Wheat malt

Pale malt forms the basis of all grain beers, therefore with these a full mash is always required.

Recipes based on malt extract will require no mashing — unless any of the additional grain does — in which case a "limited mash" is involved. Whichever method is being used, all grain, except flaked adjuncts, should be "cracked".

▼ Malt when whole (left) and cracked. Cracking the malt enables the hot water during mashing to activate the enzyme diastase. This, in turn, converts the starch content to fermentable dextrins and maltose.

CRACKING

For the contents of the grain to be extracted, the husks have to be lightly crushed or cracked. Care must be taken during this stage as over-cracking will produce too powdery a grist resulting in inefficient mashing with risk of an irreversible haze in the finished beer. Under-cracking is liable to result in too much malt remaining whole, so giving a poor extraction rate. The equipment suitable for cracking is mentioned on p. 31.

The other solution to this problem is to buy the grain ready crushed. This will normally cost slightly more, but it is well worthwhile if the alternative is to crush the grain manually. However, if you have an electric grinder or blender you may find the saving and added freshness preferable. Flaked adjuncts. do not require crushing.

MASHING

Once the malt has been crushed, it is ready to be mashed, using a suitable container such as a boiler with a tap and tight-fitting lid (see equipment). To prevent the tap getting blocked with grain, use some form of inner container, such as a muslin bag or perforated bucket resting on blocks. In the illustration, a saucepan lid, or equivalent, stops the muslin bag blocking the tap during draining. In the absence of any other means, the tap should be protected with a wooden spoon when sparging is in progress.

During mashing, the infusion of the malt and water releases the enzyme diastase, which converts the non-fermentable starch content of the grain into fermentable sugars (maltose and dextrins).

As this is the most important single operation in brewing, the utmost care needs to be taken to achieve the best results.

The grain should be mixed with the water at an approximate rate of 3 lbs to each gallon, so for example in Recipe A, two gallons of water would be used.

Temperature control

The temperature of the mixture during mashing needs to be held at 65-66°C (148-152°F). The water is there-

▼ The malt is held in a muslin sack to avoid blockage. A saucepan lid on blocks also keeps the sack clear of the tap.

Insulated by blanket

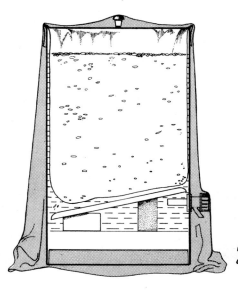

Insulated by heat bath and blanket

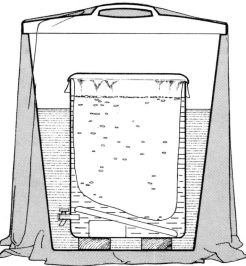

fore put into the mash tun at about 75°C (165°F). The grain is then added, stirring well to avoid any balls of grain forming and to enable even distribution of heat. During the mixing the over-all temperature should settle at about 65°C (150°F). After checking the temperature at this point, it can be adjusted with hot or cold water as necessary. It is important to have adjusting water ready at hand as the first few minutes of mashing are the most crucial.

Once the mash is at the correct temperature it needs to be maintained within the same range, 65-66°C (148-152°F) for 1½-2 hours. The means of temperature control depends upon the equipment used (see equipment section), but whether you use a heat bath, blankets or some other means of insulation, do not disturb the mash for the first 30 minutes while the chemical reactions involved are at their least stable. Then, if in doubt, check the temperature and adjust if required.

After your first experience of brewing, you should be able to organize a mash system which requires no attention after the grist has been added to the water.

Mashing should last for 1½-2 hours. This can be prolonged and, in fact, it is fairly common practice for a mash to be left overnight before sparging – the longer period, if anything, produces a superior wort. During a prolonged mash, there is no need to rectify any heat loss after the initial 1½ hour period.

Iodine test

To check that the starch content has been fully converted, take a small sample of the wort and add a few drops of iodine. If the iodine turns dark blue, it means that there is still some starch present and more mashing is required.

Lager malt

Lager malt can be mashed following the above procedure. However, if a protein haze is carried through

to the finished beer, a modified decoction mash is advisable. This means maintaining the temperature of the wort at 52°C (125°F) for 30 minutes then raising it to 66°C (150°F) for a further 1½ hours.

Limited mash

In Recipe B, the only grain used is crystal malt. As this does not require mashing, the first process after crushing the grain will be boiling. (See p.52)

Where malt extract is used with an adjunct which requires mashing, the following "limited mash" is adopted: into the vessel used for boiling add the malt extract and crushed grains to 1½-2 gallons of water. Mash at 65°C (150°F) for 45 minutes.

At the end of this period, there is no sparging or "running off" involved—the wort and spent grains are simply kept in the container for the next stage, boiling.

▼ How six gallons of water are allocated for a five gallon brew.

6 gallons of water   **2 gallons for mashing**   **4 gallons for sparging**   **5 gallon brew**

SPARGING

Once the sugars have been fully extracted in the mash tun the sugary wort must be rinsed from the spent grain. So that this is done without sugar being retained in the husks, the wort and grains need to be sparged or sprayed with hot water during the rinsing.

In former times brewers did not sparge the grains, and the sugar consequently retained in the mash tun was used for a secondary, weaker brew called "small beer".

As shown in the diagram, 4-4½ gallons of water at 75°C (165°F) (the same as the initial mash liquor temperature) is used for sparging. The process is best carried out with the equipment arranged as in the diagram — and if an electric boiler is used instead of the boiling pan illustrated, this can be heating up the wort for subsequent boiling as it is collected.

It is most important for the sparge water to be sprayed and not simply poured onto the grains. This enables the maximum amount of sugar to be taken into solution as the liquor sinks slowly down through the grains. The grains, if undisturbed, filter powdery substances from the wort which would, if retained, tend to upset the wort balance and clarity. The grains should therefore only be stirred if a blockage occurs in the draining. After the wort has been collected, the spent grain is ideal for hens or the compost heap.

▼ Sparging rinses the sugars in solution from the mass of spent grain. For efficient extraction, 4 gallons of liquor at 75°C (165°F) should be used for an average strength 5 gallon brew. This amount can be raised to a maximum rate of one gallon per pound of mashed malt grain if required.

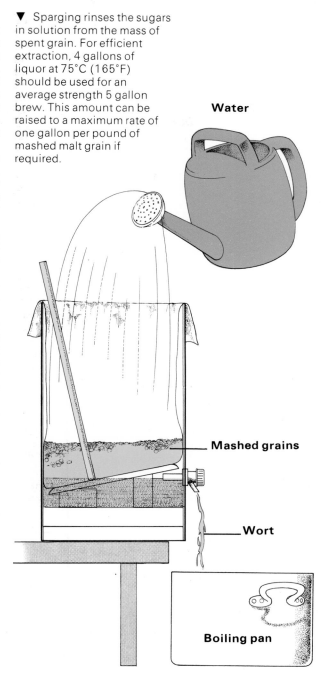

Water

Mashed grains

Wort

Boiling pan

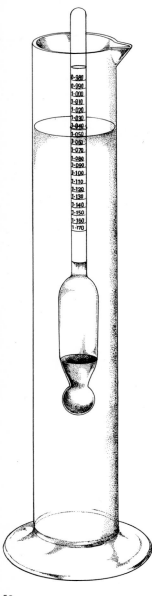

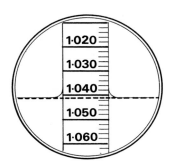

▲ Ignore the meniscus and take the reading at the surface; here 1,041 and not 1.039.

THE HYDROMETER

As sugar is the ingredient which is fermented out to alcohol in beer, an item of equipment which is able to test the sugar content of a wort will have an obvious importance to the brewer.

This rôle is filled by the hydrometer, which is used to check the amount of sugar in solution by measuring the density of the liquid.

The hydrometer is a closed glass tube consisting of a bulbous lower end and a narrow calibrated stem. The bottom half is weighted sufficiently for it to float upright in a solution. The principle of the hydrometer is that the denser a solution, the more it will support a weight placed in it. So if the hydrometer is placed in pure water, the whole stem will almost sink below the surface, but if placed in a thick solution, the stem will protrude well proud of the surface. If the stem is calibrated with water having an arbitrary value of 1.000, a liquid's density can be recorded numerically, giving a value called its specific gravity (SG).

For beer brewing, a suitable hydrometer would have a range of SGs from 1.000-1.100. Water has a specific gravity of 1.000 and beers normally range from 1.030-1.055.

When a reading is being taken, insert the hydrometer into the liquid and twist sharply between the thumb and forefinger. This releases any air which may have been trapped under the bowl or on the sides. When the hydrometer has settled, take the reading where the stem breaks the surface. You will notice that the surface of the liquid moves upward at the sides of the stem. This curve, known as the meniscus, is caused by the surface tension of the liquid and must be disregarded in any reading. Consequently the correct reading in the enlarged part of the diagram is 41 and not 39. The liquid therefore has a specific gravity of 1.041.

So that readings can be made accurately, it is advisable to use a hydrometer jar for the sample of liquid as shown.

During fermentation

Besides measuring the original density of the wort, the hydrometer is used to check the progress of fermentation. Thus it provides a safe assessment of the time when the beer is ready to be bottled and avoids the wastage that can be caused by bottling too early with the consequent risk of breakage.

As the sugar is converted by the yeast to alcohol and carbon dioxide, the density goes down, since pure alcohol is less dense than water. If fermentation has apparently ceased and the density has reached 1.010, it is safe to siphon the beer into bottles or other sealed containers. Some light beers will ferment out to a density 1.006-1.008.

A hydrometer is useful in co-ordination with records of previous brews so that any poor extraction can be spotted at the time and rectified as necessary.

Temperature adjustment

The specific gravity reading is affected by the temperature of the liquid. If a sample of wort is heated, the liquid expands and so becomes less dense. Similarly, as a liquid loses temperature, its volume contracts, resulting in a rise in density. To solve the problem of fluctuating density, the hydrometer is calibrated at a standard temperature of 15°C (59°F). So, although the standard setting is suitable for fermentation readings, some correction will be needed for measurements of gravity, for

Temperature adjustment chart

Hydrometers are calibrated at a temperature of 15°C (59°F) and throughout this book, gravity readings have been corrected to this standard. To adjust readings, multiply by the following correction factors:

°C	°F		
71	160	× reading by	2.66
66	150	,,	2.35
60	140	,,	2.06
54	130	,,	1.72
49	120	,,	1.57
43	110	,,	1.37
38	100	,,	1.27
32	90	,,	1.18
27	80	,,	1.10
21	70	,,	1.02
16	60	,,	1.00
10	50	,,	0.96

Average yield figures for the main sources of fermentable sugars.

Source	Specific Gravity (1 lb/gal)
Pale malt	30
Lager malt	30
Crystal malt	24
Malt extract	31
White sugar	38
Invert sugar	30
Demerara sugar etc.	36
Glucose chips	36
Wheat malt	30
Flaked barley	30
Flaked rice	30
Flaked maize	30

example at mashing temperatures.

Correction factors are shown in the accompanying table.

If a sample of wort has a reading of 20 at 66°C (150°F), to find the true SG, multiply by 2.35.

$$SG = 20 \times 2.35 = 47$$

If the hydrometer does not also have percentage readings, to find the alcohol content of a beer, subtract the final gravity reading from the original gravity or OG and multiply by $\frac{3}{22}$.

Initial SG = 1045
Final SG = 1010
―――
35

Difference of $35 \times \frac{3}{22}$

= 4.77 per cent alcohol.

51

Boiling, pitching and cooling

Whether the ingredients being used have required a full mash, a limited mash or no mash period at all, the next stage in a brew is to boil the wort with the hops and any sugar that is being used.

Boiling the wort is far easier if it can be carried out in one large container such as an electric boiler or boiling pan. If boiling has to be done in stages, it is preferable for the ingredients to be evenly distributed. Do not boil the hops in one container of wort and the sugar in another.

▼ A vigorously boiling wort.

BOILING

The boiling of the wort is important for the following reasons:

1 to extract the useful constituents of the hops;
2 to kill the enzymes in the wort;
3 to sterilize the wort;
4 to cause precipitation of protein matter;
5 to regulate the concentration.

For these activities to take place the wort needs to be boiled for a period of 1-$1\frac{1}{2}$ hours. If less time is taken there is the risk that insufficient protein will have been precipitated out of solution. The recommended period is also required to achieve full extraction from the hops. On the other hand, too long a boiling is likely to produce an adverse flavour—apart from being a waste of fuel.

Hops

Before adding the hops, measure them out carefully and remove any foreign matter found. Any unfinished bags of hops should be tightly resealed and stored in a cool dark place until next required. If compressed hops are being used, these are easily measured out with a ruler and sliced off.

A high proportion of the oil content of hops is evaporated off during boiling with a consequent loss in the fragrance of the finished beer. This can be offset by holding back a few hops and adding them during the last 15 minutes, although this is rather wasteful as other properties will not be extracted in such a brief period. It is preferable to add a small handful of hops at the end of fermentation — a practice known as "dry hopping".

Once the wort has reached the boil the temperature should be maintained so that there is a continuous turbulent rolling action on the surface. Gentle simmering is not sufficient.

With this in mind, it is wise to add the hops before the wort boils so that they are more manageable whilst being stirred in. Allow for the extra space taken up by the turbulence and froth when filling the container to avoid spillage.

Some home-brewers place the hops in a muslin bag and drop this into the wort with a length of string attached — in the same way that one uses a tea bag. This makes the hops easy to remove at the end. The drawback with this method is that it restricts the free movement of the hops in the wort which helps the precipitation of the protein. If the hops are loose at the end of the boiling they serve as an efficient filter bed and are also sparged more successfully.

▼ Gently stirring, add hops loose to the wort. This should be done before boiling point is reached to avoid extra turbulence.

▼ The sugar should also be added to the wort before it boils. Stir in thoroughly to avoid burning and caramelization.

Enzymes and bacteria

However successfully the mashing and sparging of the grain is undertaken, diastase enzymes (alpha and beta amylase) will still be present in the wort. Unless their activity is speedily halted, the balance of sugar (maltose to dextrin) will be altered and affect the fermentation.

Boiling the wort therefore has a further value in killing the enzyme activity. It also sterilizes the liquid, so destroying bacteria which would otherwise ruin the brew before fermentation could get under way.

Concentration

If you wish to strengthen a particular brew, the quantity of sugar can be increased. However, too much sugar will produce a thin, unpleasant beer. The alternative is to reduce the original volume of wort by prolonging the boiling (and removing the lid of the container). The higher evaporation rate will then reduce the volume and, of course, at the same time produce a darker beer. Conversely, diluting a wort to increase volume will lighten it.

Clarification

Boiling the wort also serves the purpose of removing protein matter which has been carried through from the mashing. The tannin content of the hops and the temperature combine to coagulate this fine matter in suspension and to precipitate it out of solution. The point at which this is achieved (after about one hour) is known as the "hot break".

To aid clarification, especially with high gravity light beers, protein finings can be used to advantage. Known as Irish Moss or Copper Finings, these are fining agents prepared from the seaweed Carragheen. Mix the fine powder into a paste with water and add for the last half hour.

Sugar

The other ingredient which should be added at this stage is sugar. Again, some people recommend straining the wort onto the sugar after boiling has ended, yet mixing the sugar into the boil serves the dual purpose of inverting it and sterilizing a dark variety which may not be fully refined.

Inverting the sugar is advantageous to the brewer as it is then immediately fermentable by yeast, so ensuring the wort stands inactive for the minimum time possible.

To invert sugar simply pour it into the wort with two teaspoons of citric acid. At the end of the boiling period the sugar will have inverted and two teaspoons of sodium bicarbonate or calcium carbonate will then neutralize the added acid.

As with the hops, add the sugar before the wort starts to boil and it will be easier to dissolve. Stir well to avoid any burning on the bottom of the container.

▼ Add yeast to $\frac{1}{2}$ pint of cooled wort or $\frac{1}{2}$ pint of water with 1 tablespoon of malt extract; 1 tablespoon sugar; $\frac{1}{2}$ teaspoon citric acid.

▼ Starter bottle under air-lock.

Hop sparge

Once the boiling period has been completed, the wort must be poured or drained from the boiler into the vessel to be used for fermentation. Before draining off the wort, let it stand for 30 minutes, to allow an initial drop in temperature.

Whether the wort is drained or poured, the hops retain a substantial amount of the extract. In order to release absorbed extract, the hops have to be sparged by pouring six pints (for a five gallon brew) of near boiling water over them before draining a second time. The water used in the hop sparge should bring the total up to the volume required, but top up if necessary.

Cooling

Once the draining and sparging has been completed, it is necessary to cool the wort down to the temperature required for fermentation— 16-21°C (60-70°F).

It is at this point, before the yeast has been pitched and started its work, that the wort is at risk from contamination.

It is therefore an advantage if the cooling period can be shortened by the forced cooling of the wort. The best method for the home-brewer is to use some form of a "cold bath". A bath or any container of sufficient size to hold the wort vessel will quickly bring the temperature down. Replace the water, as it warms up, with fresh cold water.

Rapid cooling also pre-cipitates yet more nitrogenous matter out of the solution, (the cold break). This improves the final clarity and prevents a very harsh taste which might otherwise occur.

Yeast starter

A yeast starter should be prepared in advance so that it is ready to be pitched in as soon as the wort has cooled to the correct temperature. In this way, the main brew is left for the minimum time before the working yeast presents a screen against infection.

To prepare the starter, add yeast to $\frac{1}{2}$ pint of cooled wort, one tablespoon of sugar, and half a teaspoon of citric acid. If the starter is sluggish, add one teaspoon of yeast nutrient.

▲ Pitching the yeast. Stir well for one minute to aerate the wort.

Pitching

With the wort at 16-21°C (60-70°F) and the yeast starter under way, you are now ready to pitch in the yeast and let it convert the brew, through fermentation, into beer.

After the yeast has been pitched and the wort roused, check that the volume is correct and note the specific gravity and temperature. Having poured the yeast in, stir briskly for one minute to aerate the brew. Cover the bin closely until the first yeast head is formed.

Fermen-tation

The amount of time that a beer will take to ferment depends on temperature, original gravity and the nature of the sugar content and yeast used.

After 8-12 hours, the first fluffy head should be starting to form on the beer, covered with a dark brown powdery matter which will need to be removed.

In 24-36 hours, the yeast will have developed a thick creamy head which should then remain throughout primary fermentation, so sealing the beer from airborne infection.

After 3-4 days, the beer is racked into an air-tight vessel where it undergoes secondary fermentation and clarification.

There are three factors which combine to produce a successful fermentation: good yeast, temperature control and cleanliness.

Yeast

Yeast is a living organism which thrives in sugary solutions. It reproduces by sub-division producing the by-products of alcohol and carbon dioxide in equal quantities.

Finding a "clean" yeast to suit your brewing may require some selection. Yeasts come in different forms such as liquid, tablet, powder and granulated, and

▼ A thick yeast head forms on a commercial beer in a fermentation tank.

they can all vary substantially in quality.

Yeast cells do not reproduce *ad infinitum,* their growth rate drops and eventually they die. Too high a percentage of weak or dead cells produces a poor yeast which will slow down fermentation, offer less protection and so increase the risk of contamination. Strains of yeast can also become infected by bacteria, a problem that can beset commercial brewers and suppliers.

If you re-use old yeast, as opposed to buying fresh for each brew, keep a continuous check on its performance and discard it as soon as there is any sign of weakening.

Top fermenting yeast

Before a top fermenting yeast throws its thick protective head the bin will need to be closely covered. Once the head is well established, the lid or covering can be removed until primary fermentation abates. As top fermenting yeasts work better with a certain amount of oxygen present, the wort can be improved by rousing daily. This is done by stirring briskly in a circular motion from top to bottom with a long-handled wooden spoon.

Rousing the wort can

also be beneficial if the attenuation is unsteady or sticking. If the crop needs skimming, this should be carried out before rousing.

As when patting or skimming the head, ensure that the spoon has been sterilized before use.

Bottom fermenting yeast

By working primarily from the bottom of the vessel, clearer brighter beers are produced with bottom fermenting yeasts. This is especially necessary for lagers, which should always be fermented using these yeasts.

Lager yeasts, as they are also called, do throw a yeast crop although it is short-lived and not as prominent as that of a top-fermenter. With this in mind care must be taken to remove the dark brown coating on the head before it sinks back into the wort. It is also advisable to keep the container covered during primary fermentation, not only for the extra protection afforded, but also as

lager yeasts do not perform as well with an aerated wort. Rousing is therefore unnecessary.

An advantage of closed fermentation is that no harm should come to a brew that is left for a day or two longer than required.

Being of pure strain, "lager yeasts" tend also to be more stable than their top fermenting counterparts.

Temperature

Lager yeasts work better at slightly lower temperatures than top yeasts. However, fermentation should generally be conducted within 12-21°C (55-70°F) and preferably as near to 15°C (60°F) as is possible.

Working within this range can sometimes be difficult for the home-brewer to achieve, especially in the summer months. Some thought should therefore be given as to the siting of the fermentation vessel. A garage in the winter or a conservatory in the summer are places to be avoided. A

▶ A commercial brewery about 1860. Cleansing tanks in which the beer was cleaned after primary fermentation and before it was placed in vats.

cellar is ideal if you have one, although most people find the cupboard under the stairs quite satisfactory.

Beer is best attenuated under constant conditions and so sharply fluctuating temperatures should be avoided.

As in most chemical processes, an increase in temperature speeds up fermentation. At first, this might appear to the energetic brewer to be a useful method of increasing his output. However, high temperatures, over 21°C (70°F), produce a racing fermentation and an unstable head. The final result is a beer with poor condition and a harsh flavour.

Too low a temperature causes fermentation to proceed sluggishly with a higher proportion of inactive cells. This will often result in the brew "sticking"

Cleanliness
As in all stages, keeping vessels and utensils in use properly clean is of the utmost importance to avoid contamination.

Primary fermentation
As mentioned previously, beer takes about seven days to ferment out (primary and secondary) depending on the original gravity and temperature.

As the yeast reproduces, the carbon dioxide gas emitted, rises through the liquid in the form of bubbles.

Some of the bubbles take up particles of yeast which are then discarded on the surface. After approximately ten hours (or up to 24 hours if no sugar has been inverted), yeast is being deposited on the surface at sufficient rate for the first fluffy yeast head to be formed. Up to this point the brew should have been closely covered for protection.

Patting the head
As well as yeast being thrown up a coating of fine dark brown particles will appear on the surface. This needs to be removed for, if it is allowed to sink back into the brew; a bitter tasting beer will be the result. The particles can be extracted either by skimming or by patting the head.

Skimming the head is slightly easier as it simply involves scooping up the upper half of the head with a spoon to remove all dark particles. Avoid removing the whole crop, although a good yeast should soon reform a head.

▼ Skim or pat the surface of the creamy yeast head to remove brown scum. Do not remove the whole head as this forms a barrier against infection.

Some poor quality yeasts will throw a head which will disintegrate almost as soon as it is formed, while others will only manage a few oily bubbles on the surface so offering no protection at all. If the crop thrown is unsatisfactory, the fault can sometimes be remedied by sprinkling one teaspoon of wine filtering powder onto the wort.

If in doubt about the performance of the yeast, instead of skimming, pat the first crop with the flat back of a wooden spoon. The brown particles will adhere to the spoon, leaving the head intact.

Any subsequent cleaning, once the head has thickened, is best done by repeating the patting operation.

When judging the performance of a yeast when brewing your own beer, you must not expect to have

▼ Fitting an air-lock to a demijohn for secondary fermentation.

such spectacular heads thrown as those seen in commercial breweries. With the quantities that they brew, the volume/surface area ratio is much higher.

Secondary fermentation

After three or four days, the primary fermentation abates and the yeast crop has to be removed by skimming before it sinks to the bottom. The beer, no longer protected by the head, needs to be protected from airborne infection by being siphoned into a vessel under air-lock. In this way, the beer is also removed from the yeast sediment so preventing the risk

of yeast bite. The air-lock works as a one way valve letting pressure escape from the beer while stopping air from entering.

Fill the container up to within 3cm of the rubber bung or cork and firmly insert the air-lock. Half fill the trap of the air-lock with water and leave the container under the same temperature conditions as applied with primary fermentation.

Secondary fermentation allows the dextrinous sugar content of the brew to be used up by the remaining yeast carried over with the beer during racking.

Once this has been completed the yeast settles out on the bottom of the container leaving the beer to partially clarify. Glass gallon jars and demijohns are useful containers for this stage so that progress can be visually checked.

As the beer under air-lock is protected from infection, a delay of a few days in final racking will do no harm. In fact, it is wiser to rack later rather than sooner so that the yeast will have bedded down into a firm sediment.

Before proceeding with racking, take a hydrometer reading to ensure that the gravity of the beer is correct.

The precise gravity reading of the beer will vary slightly at this stage depending on the type of beer and its original gravity. Racking should generally take place after the beer gives a reading of 1.008-1.010.

Clarifica-
tion

By the time the beer is ready for racking, the bulk of the yeast will have settled out of the liquid and formed a thick sediment. The beer is then siphoned off this deposit into bottles or a cask for storage.

The yeast that was still in suspension is now re-activated during storage by priming, the addition of further sugar. This final controlled fermentation builds up pressure in the beer giving it what is called its "condition".

During the remainder of the maturation period, the residual yeast precipitates out of solution leaving the beer crystal clear and ready for drinking.

In the course of brewing, you may come across someone who maintains that a cloudy beer is a truly traditional beer and that the yeast present will serve to keep you in a healthy state. Except that the yeast may be good for you, beer was never meant to look or taste "yeasty" nor should it be our intention now.

Fining agents

Beer should be able to clear perfectly well naturally without the aid of commercial fining agents. However, such finings may be required if something has gone amiss during the brewing, resulting in a yeast haze being thrown, i.e. yeast remaining in suspension. Beers which are going to be stored for some months may take up the sharp flavour of the yeast sediment over such a long period and they may also benefit from their use.

Isinglass and gelatine are the two main fining agents used in beer brewing. Isinglass can either be bought in the dried state or as a commercially prepared solution. The natural dried isinglass has the advantage of keeping indefinitely, but is difficult to dissolve and, once in solution, must be kept below 21°C (70°F). The commercially prepared solutions are much stabler and more convenient to use.

Gelatine can be bought in sachets at chemists, brewing shops or general stores. A sachet is mixed into a paste with cold water before adding to the beer and should be sufficient for fining a five gallon brew. Both fining agents will leave a beer brilliantly clear in 24-48 hours.

Paper filters are not recommended as they do not cope particularly well with beer yeast in the quantities involved, and in any case, over-expose the beer to the air.

If finings are to be used they should be mixed in two days before bottling or casking. Care must be taken to avoid over-fining which will affect the condition of the beer and might necessitate adding more yeast.

On the other hand, if being used to clear a yeast haze, slightly more finings will be required specifically to remove all the yeast. Transfer the affected beer into a fresh container. Add finings and leave closed for 48 hours. Then siphon back into the bottles or casks (well sterilized in the meantime), add fresh yeast and re-prime.

▲ Priming sugar sets off a final fermentation under pressure which produces the conditioning in the beer. Add directly to each bottle (1 teaspoon per quart) or cask ($\frac{1}{2}$ oz per gallon). This should be done immediately before racking.

The head of the beer

When a bottle of beer is opened, the higher pressure of carbon dioxide rises to the surface in bubbles. The bubbles are coated with fine matter from the liquid which combine on the surface to form a frothy head. The ability for the head to remain on the beer depends on the cleanliness of the glass used and the length of maturation, in addition to how well the beer was brewed.

To improve the head, a commercially produced heading liquid can be used. As with finings, their use is very much dependent on in-dividual taste. Using them is more warranted in lagers and stouts where a creamy head is especially required. Add the heading liquid along with any finings and hops (if dry hopping), 48 hours be-fore bottling or casking. If fined beer is to be bottled, use $\frac{1}{3}-\frac{1}{2}$ of the heading liquid dosage recommended for a draught beer.

Priming and racking

The bottles or casks that are going to hold the beer need to be primed with sugar so the residual yeast can pro-duce a final content of car-bon dioxide in solution. A beer so treated is known as "live" or "naturally condi-tioned". Before condition-ing occurs, all the carbon dioxide gas produced has to be allowed to escape leaving the beer entirely flat.

To prime, place one level teaspoon of white sugar in each quart bottle, ($\frac{1}{2}$ tea-spoon for pint bottles) using a funnel as illustrated. For casks, add $\frac{1}{2}$ oz of sugar per gallon. If the cask has a safety valve, the beer can benefit from double this figure.

With the bottles (or casks) cleaned and primed, the beer can be racked. The rate of flow is dependent upon the height of the vessel above the bottles; the great-er the height, the faster the flow. If you need to slow down or stop the beer, squeeze the siphon tube at the bottle end rather than pull the tube out of the beer.

The bottles should be filled up to 3cm below the stopper. Casks should also have space left in them as directed according to size. The most popular size of cask ($5\frac{1}{4}$ gallons) should hold no more than $4\frac{1}{2}$ gal-lons, with any beer that is left over being bottled. Simi-larly, the $2\frac{1}{4}$ gallon size should hold $1\frac{3}{4}$ gallons.

If racking is carefully car-ried out, both between fer-mentation stages and when bottling, there should be only a smear of yeast sedi-ment on the bottom of a beer bottle once it is ready for drinking. Excessive yeast carried over is liable to pro-duce a cloudy beer when poured.

▼ Racking must be done as one continuous operation. To slow down or stop the flow, pinch the siphon tube but do not remove the tube from the beer.

Storage and serving

The type of container used to store a brew will vary depending on the sort of beer and on what is readily available to the brewer.

Basically, bitters, milds and some Irish stouts are best as draught beers served from a cask, while the remainder should be bottled.

Bottles should be kept upright at a cool temperature as this aids clarification. However, kept too cold there is a risk of a haze forming. Fortunately this disappears as the temperature rises again.

▼ Unless consumed in a comparatively short space of time, beer is most manageable in bottles. Bottled beer will also have more condition and a better head. If possible, store in brown or green bottles to avoid exposure to sunlight.

1 External screw cap
2 External screw cap (e.g. lemonade bottle)
3 Crown cap
4 Threaded stopper
5 Re-usable plastic cap

BOTTLING

Preferably use beer or cider bottles for beer. They are constructed for the purpose and any drink tastes better if poured from the correct type of bottle. The common sizes for our purposes are the quart, the pint and the half pint, or their metric equivalents which are at present being phased in.

The quart and pint bottles are the popular sizes for general use but the half pint is a handy size for the time you brew a gallon of a strong brew best drunk by small measure.

For the quart flagons, use screw stoppers and for the smaller bottles crown caps or plastic re-seal caps. Discard any cracked or chipped

▲ Lever-action crown-capper.

▼ Simple tool for crown-capping. The head of the tool is placed over the crown-cap and hit lightly with a hammer.

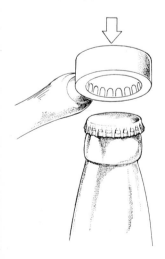

bottles and replace stopper rings as they become worn.

Always keep bottles well cleaned and sterilized. After cleaning take 1 fl oz of your stock solution of sodium metabisulphate and dilute with warm water to $\frac{1}{4}$-$\frac{1}{2}$ pint. Using a funnel, pour into your first bottle, shake well and transfer it to the next, repeating the operation down the line. This quantity will be sufficient for a five gallon batch of bottles, but must be discarded afterwards. Do not rinse the bottles until they are next going to be used for the traces of the solution left in the bottom will keep them fresh.

Once a bottle is opened, it is best to use all of the contents at the time. However if this is not practical, re-seal, leave in a cool place and after 24-48 hours the yeast will have re-settled.

Be wary when re-opening the bottle as the extra air-space will have produced a greater build-up of pressure.

Draught beer

Storing beer in a barrel or cask is convenient to the brewer as well as suiting some beers better than bottling. Bottle cleaning can be rather a tedious and time-consuming task, so making the choice of replacing bottles with one large vessel is an attractive alternative. Racking also becomes a simpler operation and the filled barrel takes up less space than the equivalent in bottles.

Plastic pressure barrels are the most popular method of storing draught beer. They are easy to clean, manageable, and fairly economical. The two sizes available are $2\frac{1}{4}$ and $5\frac{1}{4}$ gallon capacities and can be used either with the normal screw cap supplied or with a CO_2 injector unit using sparklet cartridges.

If an injector unit is not being used, the beer can be re-primed with sugar if it loses condition and pressure. A further 1-2 weeks will then be required for the beer to clarify again.

The CO_2 injector unit with safety valve has the advantage of maintaining an even pressure. There need be no concern that, by this method, an unnatural force-fed beer is produced. The beer has still been primed to condition naturally and the sparklets merely add a pressure of gas over the beer to prolong its life and facilitate pouring.

There are other similar containers now on the market which vary in quality and price, so if you are considering buying a cask, it is wise to discover what selection there is locally before deciding.

A suitably sized wooden barrel such as a pin ($4\frac{1}{2}$ gallons) is highly recommended as you will taste no beer better than that "from the wood". But be warned, being of porous rough material, wooden barrels require much attention to stay clean.

Serving

Suitable beer glasses or tankards are strongly recommended. Before use, they should be thoroughly cleaned, removing any trace of detergent which would affect the head on the beer.

As soon as a bottle is opened, the release of pressure will start to lift the yeast sediment. Beer must therefore be served carefully as shown in the diagram. Tilt the bottle slowly towards the glass and pour as illustrated. Do not raise the bottle between glasses and avoid any jerking movement which will disturb the yeast. In this way the beer can be poured to the last centimetre without clouding occurring.

In hot weather, beer can become too lively resulting in fobbing or frothing. This can be cured by opening the stopper or cap a crack to release the top volume of pressure and re-sealing before foaming occurs. Repeat this procedure daily until the beer settles to normal condition.

Records

Initially it might appear that maintaining records of brews is an unnecessary complication for the beginner. However, records are most valuable, particularly when you first start to brew, for they enable mistakes to be detected easily and avoided thereafter. It is surprising how quickly your brewing will improve if full records are kept.

Record the following:
1 Recipe used
2 Dates and times involved
3 Gravity readings
4 Notes on beer's progress

Labels

Labelling of bottles is also helpful, especially if there are different beers running at the same time. The small circular self adhesive labels are quite sufficient for recording the contents and date bottled. It is handy also to mark the first and last of each batch.

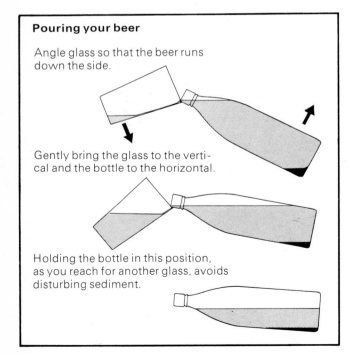

Pouring your beer

Angle glass so that the beer runs down the side.

Gently bring the glass to the vertical and the bottle to the horizontal.

Holding the bottle in this position, as you reach for another glass, avoids disturbing sediment.

Beer recipes

The following recipes are intended as a practical introduction to a range of beers and lagers. In each section there is a choice of malt extract or malt recipes so that you may choose which you prefer to use.

For the first-time brewer, it is advisable to start with the simple recipes such as those given on p.46 or try your hand with a beer kit before embarking on some of the more complicated recipes listed below.

1 Tin of malt extract
2 Dried hops
3 Granulated sugar
4 Calibrated jug
5 Spoon
6 Sachet of yeast
7 Instructions

As home-brewing has become such a popular pastime it is understandable for a wide range of beer kits to have come on the market. These enable beer to be made with a minimum of effort. In return the brewer pays for this convenience by having to spend slightly more money.

Basic kits usually contain malt extract, hops or hop preparations and a yeast. As a general rule, choose the kit which gives the most malt for the money. Avoid those which do not require boiling.

Remember that they are a convenience product and you should be able to surpass them in quality when preparing your own brews.

BITTER

The most popular of the British beers is bitter. This is basically a draught beer and home-brewers should remember this when bottling the beer and reduce the mount of sugar used in priming. Bitters are very similar to pale ale beers although they are slightly sweeter and fuller flavoured. This beer is produced in a wide range of strengths varying from an original gravity of 35-55. The quantities specified in each recipe make five gallons of beer.

Bitter 1   OG 40

5 lb pale malt
8 oz crystal malt
1 lb white sugar
3 oz Fuggles hops
Top fermenting beer yeast

Basic procedure (see p.46) Water: moderately hard. Add $\frac{1}{2}$ tsp Gypsum per gal. Mash: heat 2 gal of water at 75°C (165°F) and mix in the malt grains. Maintain the temperature for 2-3 hrs at 65-66°C (148-152°F). Boil: add hops and sugar. Boil for $1\frac{1}{4}$ hrs adding Irish Moss for last 30 mins. Fermentation: make up to the required volume of 5 gal and pitch yeast when temperature has dropped to 16-21°C (60-70°F). Allow to ferment in a cool place. Dry hop with a handful of Fuggles (20 hops approx). When the fermentation has ceased and the gravity reading is 9-10, rack into a cask or flagons. Allow three weeks for maturing in bottles or one week if in a barrel.

Bitter 2   OG 47

6 lb pale malt
8 oz crystal malt
4 oz flaked maize
1 lb demerara sugar
3 oz Goldings hops
Top fermenting beer yeast

Basic procedure (see p.46). Water: moderately hard. Adjust with pale ale water treatment where necessary. Directions as in Bitter 1.

Bitter 3   OG 45

5 lb pale malt
1 lb crystal malt
8 oz wheat malt
1 lb demerara sugar
2 oz Goldings hops
1 oz Fuggles hops
Top fermenting beer yeast
Directions as in Bitter 1.

Bitter 4   OG 43

4 lb light malt extract
1 lb crystal malt
2 lb glucose chips
3 oz Goldings hops
Bottom fermenting beer yeast

Basic procedure (see p.46). Directions as in Bitter 1.

Bitter 5   OG 48

5 lb DMS malt extract
8 oz crystal malt
4 oz wheat malt
1 lb glucose chips
$3\frac{1}{2}$ oz Goldings hops
Top fermenting beer yeast

Water: moderately hard. Adjust with Gypsum. Mash: mix grains and extract in $1\frac{1}{2}$ gal of water preheated to 75°C (165°F). Maintain at 65°C (150°F) for $\frac{3}{4}$ hr. Add hops and sugar and boil for 45-60 mins. Fermentation: make up quantity to 5 gal and cool to 16-19°C (60-65°F). Pitch with top fermenting yeast. Final racking 8-10. Allow three weeks for maturing in bottles and one week in a barrel.

Bitter 6   OG 47

5 lb DMS malt extract
8 oz crystal malt
2 lb white sugar
2 oz Goldings hops
1 oz Fuggles hops
Top fermenting beer yeast

For method see Bitter 5.

PALE ALES

A light-coloured bottled beer with more body than the light ales, pale ales are well hopped with a gravity of 45-50.

Pale Ale 1   OG 49

6 lb pale malt
8 oz crystal malt
8 oz flaked barley
1 lb white sugar
3 oz Goldings hops
Top fermenting beer yeast

Basic procedure (see p.46). Water: moderately hard. Use a pale ale water treatment (see p.45). Mash: heat 2 gal of water 71-77°C (160-170°F) and mix in grain. Mash: for 3 hrs at 66-68°C (150-155°F). Boil: add hops and sugar and boil for $1\frac{1}{2}$ hrs. Add 1 tsp of Irish Moss for last 30 mins. Fermentation: make up 5 gal and pitch yeast when cooled to 16-19°C (60-65°F). Bottle when gravity reading has settled at 10-11 and store for 4 weeks before drinking.

Pale Ale 2 OG 52

7 lb pale malt
8 oz wheat malt
1 lb demerara sugar
$3\frac{1}{2}$ oz Goldings hops
Bottom fermenting lager
   yeast

For directions see previous recipe.

Pale Ale 3 OG 49

5 lb light malt extract
4 oz crystal malt
8 oz flaked maize
$3\frac{1}{2}$ oz Goldings hops
Beer yeast

Basic procedure (see p.46). Water: moderately hard. Add 1 tsp Gypsum and 1 tsp Epsom salts. Mash: add grains and extract to $1\frac{1}{2}$ gal of water and maintain at a temperature of 66°C (150°F) for 1 hr. Boil: add hops and sugar and boil for a further 60 mins adding 1 tsp of Irish Moss for last 30 mins. Fermentation: make up to required quantity and pitch yeast when wort has cooled to 65°F. Final racking at gravity reading 9-10. Bottle and leave for 4 weeks.

LIGHT ALES

Light bodied and refreshing, this beer has a fairly low alcohol content and is always bottled. It is quite highly carbonated and should have good head retention.

Light Ale 1 OG 36

4 lb pale malt
4 oz crystal malt
$1\frac{1}{2}$ lb white sugar
2 oz Goldings hops
Top fermenting yeast

Basic procedure (see p.46). Water: treat with 1 tsp Gypsum and 1 tsp Epsom salts. Mash: heat 2 gal to 75°C (165°F), add grains and maintain temperature at 66°C (150°F) for $1\frac{1}{2}$-2 hrs. Boil: add hops and sugar and boil for 1 hr. Fermentation: make up to 5 gal and pitch top fermenting yeast when cooled to 19-21°C (65-70°F). Final racking at gravity reading 8-10. Leave bottled for 2 weeks before tasting.

Light Ale 2 OG 40

5 lb pale malt
4 oz crystal malt
8 oz flaked barley
1 lb invert sugar
$2\frac{1}{4}$ oz Goldings hops
Lager yeast

Basic procedure (see p.46). Water: moderately hard. Use pale ale water crystals. Mash: maintain temperature 65-66°C (150-152°F) for 2-3 hrs. Boil: add hops and boil for $1\frac{1}{4}$-$1\frac{1}{2}$ hrs. Strain on to sugar and cool to 16°C (60°F) before pitching a bottom fermenting lager yeast. Final racking at gravity reading 8-10. Store 3 weeks before drinking.

Light Ale 3 OG 39

4 lb DMS malt extract
12 oz wheat malt
$1\frac{1}{2}$ lb white sugar
2 oz Goldings hops
Top fermenting yeast

Basic procedure (see p.46). Water: moderately hard. Use pale ale water treatment. Mash: pour grains and malt into $1\frac{1}{2}$ gal of water and keep for 45 mins at 66°C (150°F). Boil: strain off, add hops and sugar and boil for $1\frac{1}{2}$ hrs. Add 1 tsp of Irish Moss for last 30 mins. Make up to 5 gal and pitch yeast when temperature has dropped to 19°C (65°F). Final racking at gravity reading 8-10. Store for 2-3 weeks before drinking.

LAGERS

Normally a very pale coloured beer, lager is a heavily carbonated drink that needs to be served chilled either on draught or from the bottle. Lager has a low hopping rate with gravity ranging from 35-45 for normal home-brewing.

Lager 1 OG 39

5 lb lager malt
8 oz flaked barley
1 lb white sugar
2 oz Hallertau hops
Lager yeast

Basic procedure (see p.46). Water: boil 6 gal for 15 mins. Add 1 tsp Gypsum. Mash: heat 2 gal of water to 71°C (160°F) and mix in the grains. Maintain a temperature of 66°C (150°F) for $2\frac{1}{2}$ hrs. Boil: add hops and sugar with 1 tsp of salt and boil for $1\frac{1}{2}$ hrs. Add Irish Moss for last 30 mins. Fermentation: make up to 5 gal and add 2 tsp of citric acid. When cooled to 16-19°C (60-65°F) pitch in a bottom fermenting yeast and allow fermentation to proceed in a closed container. Final racking at gravity reading 8-10. Allow 4 weeks to mature.

Lager 2   OG 39

5 lb pale malt
8 oz flaked maize
1 lb white sugar
$2\frac{1}{2}$ oz Saaz hops
Lager yeast

For method see previous recipe.

If heading liquid is used for either recipe, add to fermentation 48 hrs before final racking. Use $\frac{1}{3}$ of the quantity if the lager is to be bottled.

Lager 3   OG 35

5 lb lager malt
1 lb flaked maize
8 oz crystal malt
$2\frac{1}{2}$ oz Hallertau hops
Lager yeast

For method see Lager 1.

Lager 4   OG 42

4 lb DMS malt extract
8 oz crystal malt
2 lb white sugar
3 oz Hallertau hops
Lager yeast

Basic procedure (see p.46)
For method see Lager 1.

Lager 5   OG 42

6 lb light malt extract
1 lb flaked maize
2 oz Hallertau hops
Lager yeast

Water: soft water treatment or boil total required volume for 15 mins. Mash: add extract and grains to $1\frac{1}{2}$ gal water and mash for 1 hr at 66°C (150°F). Boil: add hops and sugar with 1 tsp salt and boil for 45 mins. Fermentation: strain into fermentation vessel and make up the volume to 5 gal. Cool to 19-21°C (65-70°F) and add yeast starter. Cover loosely until fermentation is under way and then fit fermentation lock. Rack primary fermentation into similar vessel. Final racking at gravity reading 9-10. Prime bottles and allow 4 weeks to mature. Serve chilled.

MILD ALES

Although not commonly made by the home-brewer, this is a pleasant sweet drink always served in draught form. It has a lower alcohol content than other beers and for our purposes will normally have a starting gravity of 35-40.

Mild Ale 1   OG 38

5 lb DMS malt extract
$\frac{1}{2}$ lb crystal malt
1 lb glucose chips
3 oz Fuggles hops
Beer yeast

Basic procedure (see p.46). Water: treat with 1 tsp salt and 1 tsp citric acid. Add cracked grain and extract to 2 gal of water along with the hops. Boil: $1\frac{1}{2}$ hrs. Stir in glucose chips to dissolve. Fermentation: make up quantity to 5 gal, cool to 19-21°C (65-70°F) and pitch with beer yeast. Final racking 9-10. Leave casked for 7 days.

Mild Ale 2   OG 38

5 lb pale malt
$\frac{1}{2}$ lb roast malt
1 lb demerara sugar
3 oz Fuggles hops
Beer yeast

Basic procedure (see p.46). Water: treat with 1 tsp salt and 1 tsp citric acid. Mash: heat 2 gal to 75°C (165°F) and stir in grains. Keep for 2 hrs at 66°C (150°F). Boil: add hops and sugar, boil for $1\frac{1}{2}$ hrs. Fermentation: make up to 5 gal. Pitch yeast when cooled to 19-21°C (65-70°F). Final racking 9-10.

Mild Ale 3   OG 37

$4\frac{1}{2}$ lb pale malt
$\frac{1}{4}$ lb black malt
$\frac{1}{2}$ lb flaked maize
1 lb demerara sugar
$2\frac{1}{2}$ oz Fuggles hops
Beer yeast

Basic procedure (see p.46). Water: soften with mild ale water treatment. Mash: hold for 2 hrs at 66°C (150°F). Iodine test. Boil: add hops and sugar. Boil $1\frac{1}{2}$ hrs. Fermentation: make up to required quantity of 5 gal and pitch yeast starter when cooled to 19°C (65°F). Rack at 7-8 and store 7 days in cask.

▶ The traditional "ploughman's lunch" of bread and cheese is served at most pubs. Accompanied by home-made beer, it makes an excellent lunch at home, too.

type stouts which can equally as well be served "from the wood". Stouts have a fairly high alcohol content with an original gravity of 45-55 but have a comparatively low hopping rate.

Stout 1   OG 49
5 lb pale malt
8 oz crystal malt
1 lb black malt
2 lb demerara sugar
3 oz Fuggles hops
Beer yeast

Basic procedure (see p.46). Water: soft. Add 1 tsp salt and 1 tsp citric acid.
Mash: heat 2 gal of water to 75°C (165°F) and stir in the grains. Leave for $2-2\frac{1}{2}$ hrs at 65-66°C (148-152°F). Boil: add hops and sugar and boil for $1\frac{1}{4}-1\frac{1}{2}$ hrs. Fermentation: make up to 5 gal, cool to 19°C (65°F) and pitch a top fermenting beer yeast. Final racking: rack into bottles when gravity has settled at 10-12, priming with 1 tsp of white sugar per quart flagon. Store for 4 weeks before tasting.

Stout 2   OG 54
7 lb pale malt
$1\frac{1}{4}$ lb roast malt
1 lb white sugar
12 oz lactose
$3\frac{1}{2}$ oz Fuggles hops
Beer yeast

Basic procedure (see p.46). Water: moderately soft. Boil total volume required for $\frac{1}{2}$ hr. Directions as for previous recipe. After the mash has been completed, use 2 pints of the wort to dissolve the lactose. This

Basic procedure (see p.46). Water: soften with mild ale water treatment. Mash: Heat 2 gal at 75°C (165°F) and mix in grains. Maintain for 2 hours 65-66°C (150-152°F). Boil: boil $1\frac{1}{2}$ hrs having added hops and sugar. Fermentation: make up to 5 gal and pitch yeast, when cooled to 19°C (65°F). Aerate by stirring vigorously. Store 3-4 weeks before sampling.

Brown Ale 4   OG 47
5 lb pale malt
1 lb black malt
2 lb demerara sugar
3 oz Fuggles hops
12 oz lactose
Beer yeast

Basic procedure (see p.46). Water: add 1 tsp salt. After mash period, use 1-2 pints of the wort to dissolve the lactose (a non fermentable sugar). This solution can then be added to the next stage for boiling with the hops and demerara sugar. Other directions as in Brown Ale 3.

Brown Ale 5   OG 52
6 lb pale malt
10 oz black malt
2 lb demerara sugar
1 oz Northern Brewer hops
2 oz Fuggles hops
Beer yeast

Directions as in Brown Ale 3.

STOUT
Stout is similar to brown ale in being a heavy bodied dark beer which is always bottled —except in the case of Irish-

BROWN ALES
Brown ale is similar to mild ale in sweetness and colour. However, brown ale is a heavy bodied drink, always bottled, and with a high alcohol content.

Brown Ale 1   OG 46
4 lb DMS malt extract
1 lb crystal malt
$\frac{1}{2}$ lb black malt
2 lb demerara sugar
3 oz Fuggles hops

Basic procedure (see p.46). Water: treat with 2 tsp salt and 2 tsp citric acid. Mash: mix grains and extract for $\frac{3}{4}$ hr at 66°C (150°F) in $1\frac{1}{2}$ gal of water. Boil: add hops and sugar and boil for 1 hr. When cooled to 19-21°C (60-65°F), pitch with a top fermenting yeast. Final racking at 10-11 and store 3 weeks before drinking.

Brown Ale 2   OG 47
3 lb malt extract superflavex
1 lb crystal malt (cracked)
$\frac{1}{2}$ lb black malt
3 lb demerara sugar
$2\frac{1}{2}$ oz Fuggles hops
$\frac{1}{2}$ oz Goldings hops
Beer yeast

Basic procedure (see p.46). Water: treat with mild ale water treatment. Other directions as above in Brown Ale 1.

Brown Ale 3   OG 48
6 lb pale malt
8 oz crystal malt
8 oz roast malt
1 lb white sugar
2 oz Fuggles hops
Beer yeast

can then be added with the other ingredients at the boiling stage.

Stout 3   OG 50
(Irish type)
6 lb pale malt
1 lb black malt
10 oz flaked maize
1 lb white sugar
2 oz Northern Brewer hops
   or 3 oz Fuggles hops
Beer yeast

Basic procedure (see p.46). Water: moderately soft. Boil total volume of water required for $\frac{1}{4}$ hr and add 1 tsp of salt. Directions as for previous 2 recipes. It is recommended for this recipe to use a proprietary heading liquid. Add the amount indicated 2 days before the final racking. If bottling, only use $\frac{1}{4}$-$\frac{1}{3}$ of the amount suggested for draught beer.

Stout 4   OG 45
5 lb DMS malt extract
12 oz pale malt
1 lb black malt
1 lb demerara sugar
12 oz lactose
$3\frac{1}{2}$ oz Fuggles hops
Beer yeast

Basic procedure (see p.46). Water: moderately soft. Add 1 tsp salt and 1 tsp of citric acid. Mash: mix grains and extract in $1\frac{1}{2}$ gal of water for 1 hr along with the salt and citric acid. Maintain the temperature at 66°C (150°F) during this period. Boil: add the hops and sugar and boil for a further hour. Fermentation: make up the required quantity with treated water and cool to 16-19°C

(60-65°F) before pitching the yeast. Rack when the gravity has settled out at 10-12 and store for 4 weeks.

Stout 4   OG 46
(Irish type)
4 lb DMS malt extract
10 oz flaked barley
1 lb black malt
$2\frac{1}{2}$ lb demerara sugar
2 oz Northern Brewer hops
Beer yeast

▲ A print of a jolly 16th-century beer-drinker.

Directions as in previous recipe. Heading liquid is again advantageous with this beer—see last paragraph in the other Irish Stout recipe (Stout 3).

Mock beers

Although true beer is based on malt and hops, there is a variety of other beverages which, being of low alcoholic content in comparison to wines and spirits, are also termed beers. The production of these "mock beers" from a wide range of ingredients is always an enjoyable pursuit—being quick and easy to make and producing a pleasant variety in taste and flavour. The first two recipes that follow—mead (honey based) and cider (apple based)—do not, strictly speaking, fall either into the beer or the mock beer category. However they are strongly recommended, both being excellent drinks. The recipes that follow are for one gallon.

Mead

4 lb honey
$\frac{1}{4}$ oz citric acid
2 tbs of freshly made tea or
1 tsp grape tannin
Brewer's yeast
Yeast nutrient

Bring half a gallon of water to the boil, stir in honey and simmer for 30 mins. When cool enough, transfer to the fermentation vessel and add a further 4 pints of water (previously boiled) with the citric acid and tea or the tannin. Allow to cool to 19-21°C (65-70°F) and add the yeast with nutrient.

After the main fermentation (7-10 days) rack into gallon container and add air-lock. When fermentation has ended rack into bottles and store. Leave at least 12 weeks before sampling.

Cider

3 lb apples (preferably mixed)
$1\frac{1}{2}$ lb white sugar or
2 lb golden syrup
Yeast and nutrient

Wash the apples and cut out any bad parts. Place in a bucket and beat into a pulp with a strong pole. Crush the pulp in a juice extractor or preferably, if you can obtain one, use a fruit press. Dissolve the sugar or golden syrup in as little water as possible (1-1$\frac{1}{2}$ pints) and add to the juice. Place in a polythene bucket and add one crushed Campden tablet with the yeast (preferably not a wine yeast) and make the quantity up to one gallon. After 10 days transfer to a one gallon jar under air-lock. When fermentation has ended bottle and leave a minimum of 6 weeks.

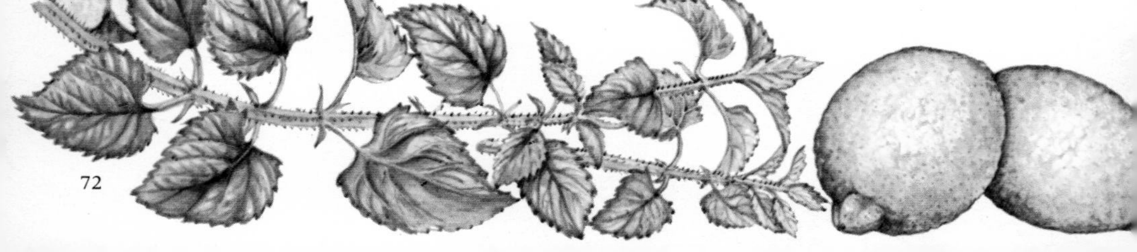

Nettle Beer
½ gal of young stinging
   nettle tops
1 lb dark malt extract
8 oz demerara sugar
1 oz hops
¼ oz root ginger (crushed)
Juice of 1 lemon
Yeast and nutrient

Wash the young nettle tops and put them into a boiler with one gallon of water, the hops, malt and ginger. Bring to the boil and simmer for 15 mins. Put the sugar and lemon juice into the fermenting vessel and strain on the liquid, stirring to dissolve. When cooled to 19-21°C (65-70°F) add yeast and nutrient and leave covered to ferment. Proceed with fermentation as with beers. Bottle and leave for 3 weeks before drinking.

Elderflower Ale
1 pint elderflowers
1 lb sugar
Juice of 1 lemon
Dried yeast and nutrient

Collect one pint of elderflowers (not pressed down), place them in a large saucepan with the juice of the lemon and the sugar and cover with boiling water. Remove from the heat, cover with a towel and leave overnight. Pour into fermentation vessel, make up to one gallon with cold water and add yeast and nutrient. Ferment out (approx. 7 days), then strain and siphon into bottles. Leave bottled for 2 weeks.

Bran Beer
8 oz bran
¾ oz hops
12 oz demerara sugar
½ tsp gravy browning
Yeast and nutrient

Boil up half a gallon of water, add bran and simmer for 1½ hrs. Stir in the hops and demerara sugar for the last 30 mins. Pour 4 pints cold water into the fermenting vessel and strain in the mixture. When cooled to 19-21°C (65-70°F) add yeast plus nutrient and proceed as with other beers. Leave bottled for 2-3 weeks.

Spruce Ale
1 lb light malt extract
1 tbs spruce essence
Juice of 1 lemon
Yeast and nutrient

Boil one gallon of water and stir in the malt extract until dissolved. Transfer to your fermentation vessel and add the spruce essence and lemon juice. Cool to 19-21°C (65-70°F) and add yeast plus the nutrient then cover and proceed with fermentation as with beer. Leave bottled for 2 weeks. Spruce essence is available from chemists and brewing shops.

Parsnip Beer
3 lb parsnips
1 lb malt extract
12 oz demerara sugar
1 oz hops
Brewer's yeast and nutrient

Scrub and slice the parsnips. Boil up one gallon of water and add the parsnips, malt extract, hops and sugar. Simmer for 30 mins stirring well then strain into fermentation vessel. Cool to 19-21°C (65-70°F) and add yeast with nutrient. Cover and allow to ferment out. After bottling, leave at least 2 weeks.

Ginger Beer
1 oz root ginger
1 lb white sugar
½ oz tartaric acid
Juice of 1 lemon
Yeast and nutrient

Crush the ginger well and add the sugar, lemon juice and tartaric acid. Bring one gallon of water to the boil and pour over ingredients. Stir well to dissolve the sugar then leave covered to cool to 21°C (70°F) before adding the yeast and nutrient. Cover well and leave for 48 hrs at 19-21°C (65-70°F). Strain into bottles and store in a cool place for 3 days before drinking.

Cooking with beer

Cooking with wine tends to be an extravagant treat saved for those special occasions, but this needn't be the case with beer. Beer is so much cheaper, especially home-brewed beer, you can use it in your cooking with some abandon. Its surprisingly subtle flavouring does not mask the true taste of the meat and it makes excellent sauces and gravies. It should not be overlooked that beer is an excellent drinking accompaniment to the following recipes.

In all these recipes great care must be taken that the beer is not allowed to evaporate as this will spoil the taste. It is advisable, therefore, to simmer rather than boil as soon as boiling point is reached.

Where beer is used in sauces or in gravy 1-2 tsps of sugar may be added, especially in the case of bitter or stout.

▼ Danish beer and bread soup.

Danish beer and bread soup
10 slices wholewheat bread
10 thin slices pumpernickel or rye bread
4 cups water
1 quart malt beer
6 tbs sugar
$\frac{1}{4}$ tsp salt
$1\frac{1}{2}$ in stick cinnamon
$\frac{1}{2}$ tsp grated lemon rind
$\frac{1}{2}$ cup double cream

Soak the bread in water overnight. When you are ready to make the soup place the soaked bread in a heavy pan over a low heat. Cook covered, stirring frequently, until it forms a thick paste. Next add beer, sugar, salt, cinnamon stick and grated lemon rind. Bring soup to the boil and cook for 5 mins. Pour into serving bowls and garnish with whipped cream. Serves 4-6.

This soup is served in Denmark on Saturday mornings instead of porridge or as an evening supper dish with herrings and anchovies. A similar soup is served in Bavaria with plenty of black pepper replacing the cinnamon and sauerkraut as garnish instead of cream'

Beef in beer

1 lb stewing steak, skirt or chuck
1 oz flour
1 oz butter
2 large onions, sliced
Salt and pepper
1 tsp brown sugar
grated nutmeg
1 garlic clove
1 bay leaf
$\frac{1}{4}$ pint beef stock
$\frac{1}{2}$ pint stout

Preheat oven to 135°C (275°F) (Gas mark 1). Cut meat into 5cm (2in) pieces and toss in flour. Melt the butter in a saucepan or casserole and add onions. Add the meat and brown on all sides. Season the meat and the onions and then add sugar, nutmeg, crushed garlic and bay leaf. Add stock and stout to the meat. Simmer in a casserole with a well-fitting lid for $2\frac{1}{2}$-3 hrs or until meat is very tender, Serve with carrots and noodles. Serves 4.

Beer caudle

1 quart of gruel made by combining some fine oatmeal with "good" beer to desired consistency
$\frac{1}{2}$ tsp allspice
$\frac{1}{3}$ tsp ground ginger
Moist sugar

Mix the oatmeal and beer and turn into a saucepan. Add the allspice and ginger and sweeten to taste with the moist sugar. Stir the gruel over a gentle heat until it is thick and cooked. Serve. Serves 4-6.

▼ Beef in beer

Sausage casserole

1 lb sausages
1 lb apples
2 large onions
$\frac{1}{2}$ tsp pepper
3 peppercorns
2 bay leaves
1 pint lager (approx.)

Grill sausages and place in casserole. Cover with alternate layers of apple and onion and season with pepper. Add the peppercorns and the bay leaves, cover with lager and bake in the oven at 175°C (350°F) (Gas mark 4) for 30 mins. Serve with roast potatoes. Serves 4.

Les Carbonnades Flamandes

(an alternative recipe for steak stewed with beer)
2 lb chuck steak
8 tbs flour
3 tsp salt
$\frac{1}{4}$ tsp pepper
2 oz dripping
1 lb onions, sliced
$\frac{3}{4}$ pint beer
1 clove garlic, chopped
Bouquet garni
1 tsp sugar
2 tbs vinegar
$\frac{1}{4}$ lb mushrooms

Cut the steak in slices about 1 cm ($\frac{1}{2}$in) thick and 5cm (2ins) square. Coat them well in the flour, salt and pepper. Fry the meat in the fat until brown. Transfer to casserole (or large pan if you prefer to cook the stew on top of the stove) and fry the onions. Add the rest of the flour and mix well. Pour

◄ Sausage casserole.

the beer into the frying-pan and stir until it boils. Pour over the meat and add the garlic, bouquet garni and sugar. Cover and cook slowly for 2-3 hrs. Add the mushrooms for the last half an hour of cooking and the vinegar just before serving. Serve with boiled potatoes and a seasonal vegetable e.g. green beans, parsnip, turnip, carrot or fried celery. Serves 4-6.

Carbonnade of beef in beer is the Belgian national dish. Any brown stew based on beef, venison, hare or chicken can be made by substituting beer for all or part of the stock or water in the stew recipe. You can experiment for yourself with different kinds of beer.

Kidneys in Irish stout

1 lb lambs' kidneys
1 lb onions
$\frac{1}{2}$ lb tomatoes
$\frac{1}{4}$ lb mushrooms
1 green pepper
Salt and pepper
1 clove garlic
1 pinch each of marjoram, parsley, rosemary and oregano *or*
1 tsp mixed herbs
$\frac{1}{2}$ pint stout
Fat or oil
Flour

Cut kidneys into 5cm (2in) square pieces and roll in the flour, herbs and seasoning. Melt the fat in a large frying pan and fry the onions until they are golden brown. Add the meat and fry for a few minutes (also until brown). Gradually stir in half the beer and simmer, making

sure all flour lumps have disappeared. Add the diced tomatoes, pepper and mushrooms, as well as the finely chopped garlic. Simmer for a further 20 mins, add the rest of the beer and cook for 5 mins until the whole dish is heated through. Serve with boiled or fried rice.

Rich roast lamb

1 leg lamb
1-2 clove(s) garlic
$\frac{1}{2}$ pint stout
$\frac{1}{4}$ lb mushrooms

Make up to a dozen slits in the lamb with a sharp kitchen knife. Cut the garlic into slivers and press into the slits (no other seasoning is necessary). Place meat in an uncovered roasting tray with half the stout and cook at 160-175°C (325-350°F) (Gas—3) allowing 45 mins per lb. 15 mins before serving pour in the remaining beer. On serving, excess liquid can be used to make a gravy by the roux method if required. Serves 4-6.

Leg of lamb is also delicious when barbecued using beer as the basting liquid.

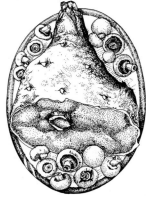

Problems and remedies

Brewing beer is an easy process for which a mixture of care and commonsense should guarantee success. Having said that, it is highly probable that, sooner or later, some problem will arise which will threaten a brew.

Some common faults are listed below which will hopefully enable you to spot the problem when it arises and to correct it in time. Once again, the importance of keeping records cannot be over-estimated as an aid in this respect.

LOW EXTRACT

This can be caused by:

Undercrushing of grain

This leaves husks of grain whole, preventing the starch and enzymes from being released.

Overcrushing

This results in too powdery a malt which will form a paste at the bottom of the mash tun inhibiting the flow of wort.

Too short a mash period: temperature

Too high a temperature can destroy the enzymes which convert the starch to fermentable sugars. The strike heat is too high for the enzymes so, as the grains and water are mixed, they must be quickly and thoroughly stirred for one minute to achieve the correct overall mashing temperature. Too low a temperature will produce an incorrect balance of sugars.

Sparging

If the wort is not sparged sufficiently, extract will be retained by the spent grain. Too harsh a sparge, i.e. pouring the water instead of spraying, will also produce an inefficient extraction.

FERMENTATION

Sticking

This can occur if a poor yeast has been used or if the temperature drops below 10-12°C (50-55°F). If the former is suspected, add some yeast nutrient and rouse the brew twice daily to keep it well aerated.

Do not add a different yeast to the brew in an effort to get it under way. The two strains may be incompatible and produce poor quality and flavour in the finished beer.

Fermentation can also stick if an air-tight lid is placed on the bin during primary fermentation. This can also result in a nauseous smell being given off from the beer. A lid or towel loosely placed over the bin is quite sufficient until the protective head is formed and indeed there is no harm done if the loose covering is left on throughout the first stage.

Racing fermentation

This can be a common problem in the summer months when a working temperature of 16-19°C (60-65°F) can be difficult to maintain. Over 25°C (77°F) fermentation will proceed with alarming speed and, unfortunately, the quality of the beer will be correspondingly impaired.

The first rule therefore is to find a place where a constant temperature of 16-19°C (60-65°F) can be kept throughout primary and secondary fermentation. However, if the problem does arise, dissolve a Campden tablet in a little water and stir in to the brew. This will cause attenuation to slow down and help to suppress any bacteria that may be activated by the high temperature.

DISEASE

Diseased beer should be rarely encountered by the home-brewer if proper attention is paid to keeping equipment clean and sterilized. There are however airborne organisms which can infect the beer. The two most common culprits are acetic acid bacteria and wild yeasts.

Acetic acid

A bacteria sometimes carried by the "vinegar fly" produces this acid, and any brew left exposed to the air is liable to attack. Results in a vinegary smell and taste to the beer.

Wild yeast

If beer is infected by airborne wild yeasts, a white powdery matter will start to appear on the surface. This will eventually spread to form a crinkled skin of quite alarming appearance.

Any diseased beer must be immediately discarded and all utensils involved, sterilized with bleach solution to avoid any recurrence of infection.

HAZES

Yeast haze

Beer should clear naturally with the yeast dropping out of suspension after all the fermentable sugar has been consumed. A poor strain of yeast may however remain in suspension, in which case the beer will need to be artificially clarified by the use of finings.

Add the correct amount of finings as directed and leave for 48 hours. This will allow time not only for the yeast to come out of suspension but also for it to bed down into a firm sediment which will not be disturbed when the beer is siphoned off. Siphon the beer into a fresh container, add new yeast and re-prime.

Protein haze

A protein haze is caused by too high a nitrogen content in the beer. This can arise at various stages in the brewing process and accordingly it can be difficult to track down the cause. A protein haze can form from:

1. Over-sparging.
2. Under-boiling.
3. Wort cooling too slowly.

After both mashing and boiling, nitrogen matter will be retained by the grain and hops respectively. If these are then over-sparged, there is the risk of the nitrogen being carried through in the wort.

Any nitrogen content retained in the wort should be precipitated out of solution by the tannin content of the hops during boiling. Insufficient boiling will weaken this activity.

Final clarification is achieved by the wort being rapidly cooled. The longer the cooling process, the less successful this precipitation will be, apart from increasing the risk of infection.

A haze can also be formed if too short a mash period is employed, resulting in starch remaining unconverted. The starch content will not only lower the extraction rate but can also cloud the finished beer.

Chill haze

Sometimes, if beer is stored at too low a temperature, a haze will be thrown. Beers and lagers stored in a refrigerator are prone to this problem. Fortunately the haze is reversible and will disappear as the temperature rises. This appears to originate from over-sparging of the hops after boiling.

FLAT BEER

Flatness is caused by a lack of conditioning in the finished beer and can result from any of the following factors:

1. Gas escaping. (Check that no bottles are cracked or chipped and that the stoppers are in good condition, forming a tight seal.)
2. Insufficient priming sugar added to the beer.
3. Bottles opened early, while the beer is still immature.
4. Beer stored at too low a temperature during storage.
5. Over-fined beer or too long a secondary fermentation period. (Rectify by pouring all beer back into a bin and add a yeast starter based on one teaspoon of yeast. Dissolve in the total amount of priming sugar required, stir well and re-bottle.)

SOUR BEER

This is normally a result of beer being stored in bottles or casks that have not been thoroughly cleaned. The yeast smell from dregs left a few days in a closed bottle will confirm the need for bottle washing.

Any sterilizing solution left in bottles, while standing empty, should also be rinsed out to avoid the risk of a "sulphur" taste occurring.

Top-fermented beer can also develop a nauseous smell if held in a tightly covered bin during primary fermentation.

World production and consumption

		Consumption 1974		Production 1974
		gals per head	Total 000's gals	Total 000's gals
1	USSR	5	1,117,600	1,117,600
2	China	—	—	38,500
3	Japan	7	799,634	796,532
4	Philippines	2	90,530	91,718
5	Australia	31	413,996	421,278
6	New Zealand	28	84,480	86,020
7	Canada	19	419,911	431,798
8	USA	18	3,723,875	183,344
9	Mexico	7	421,982	19,831
10	Columbia	8	186,252	8,464
11	Brazil	3	267,454	12,157
12	Argentina	4	100,716	4,578
13	Turkey	1	25,102	1,177
14	Europe	19	6,931,653	7,090,197

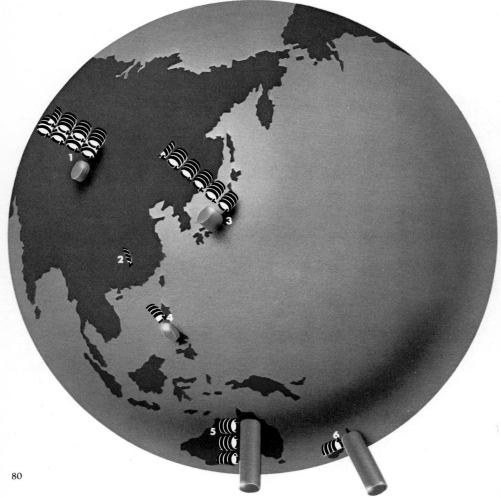

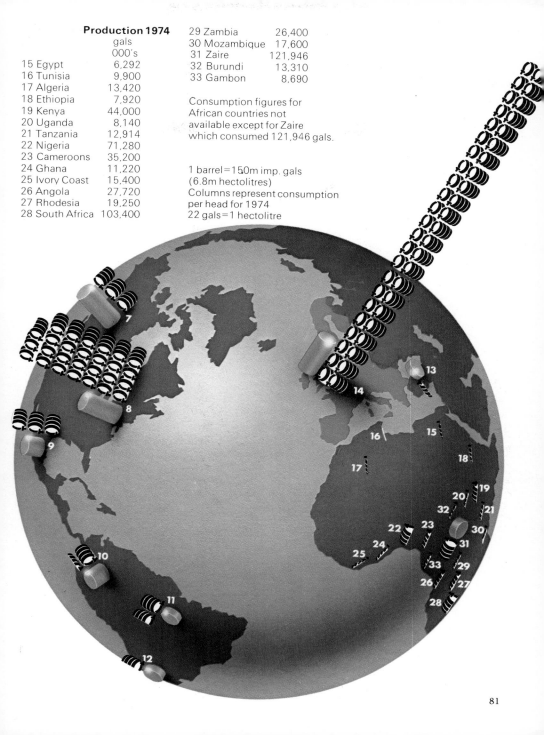

Production 1974

gals
000's

15	Egypt	6,292
16	Tunisia	9,900
17	Algeria	13,420
18	Ethiopia	7,920
19	Kenya	44,000
20	Uganda	8,140
21	Tanzania	12,914
22	Nigeria	71,280
23	Cameroons	35,200
24	Ghana	11,220
25	Ivory Coast	15,400
26	Angola	27,720
27	Rhodesia	19,250
28	South Africa	103,400
29	Zambia	26,400
30	Mozambique	17,600
31	Zaire	121,946
32	Burundi	13,310
33	Gambon	8,690

Consumption figures for
African countries not
available except for Zaire
which consumed 121,946 gals.

1 barrel=150m imp. gals
(6.8m hectolitres)
Columns represent consumption
per head for 1974
22 gals=1 hectolitre

Europe: production and consumption

1 barrel=100m gals
(4.5m hectolitres)
Columns represent consumption
per head for 1974
22 gals=1 hectolitre

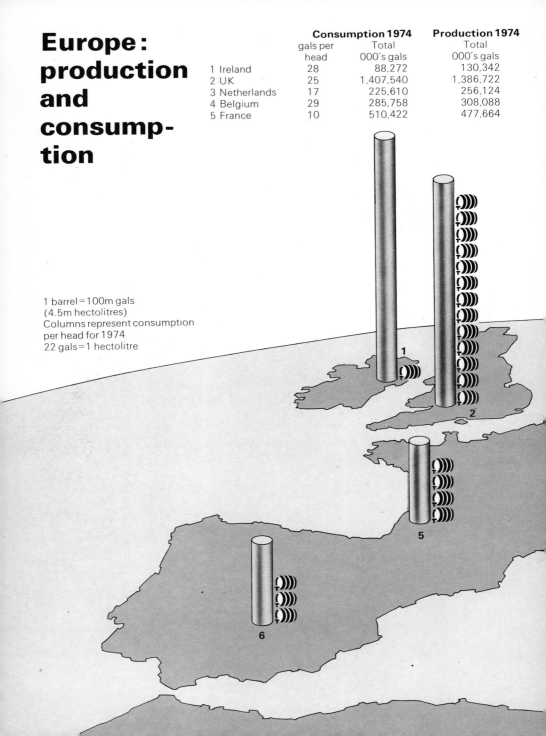

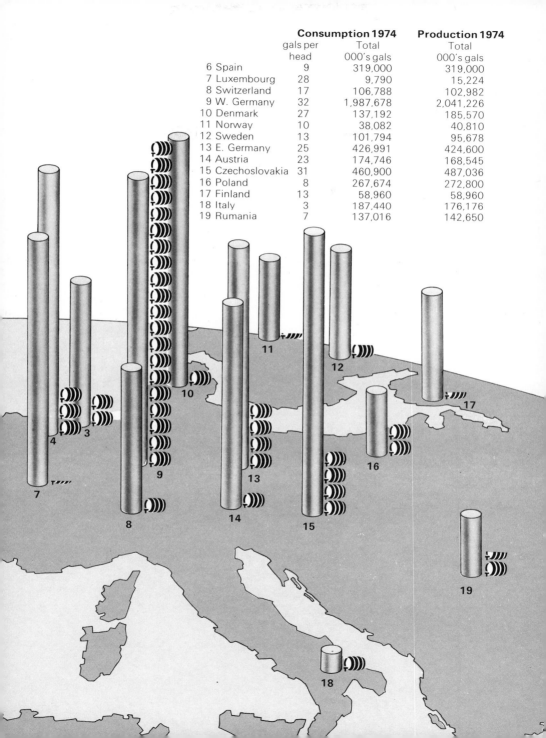

| | Consumption 1974 | | Production 1974 |
	gals per head	Total 000's gals	Total 000's gals
6 Spain	9	319,000	319,000
7 Luxembourg	28	9,790	15,224
8 Switzerland	17	106,788	102,982
9 W. Germany	32	1,987,678	2,041,226
10 Denmark	27	137,192	185,570
11 Norway	10	38,082	40,810
12 Sweden	13	101,794	95,678
13 E. Germany	25	426,991	424,600
14 Austria	23	174,746	168,545
15 Czechoslovakia	31	460,900	487,036
16 Poland	8	267,674	272,800
17 Finland	13	58,960	58,960
18 Italy	3	187,440	176,176
19 Rumania	7	137,016	142,650

Beers around the world

In 1973, world beer production was 15 times that of a century earlier. Though beer drinking has increased steadily in the old-established brewing centres of Europe and North America, much of the expansion has occurred in Asia, Africa and South America. Japan, for instance, now has a large and highly sophisticated brewing industry. Nevertheless, the average Central and Northern European still consumes more beer than anyone else. As the maps on the previous pages show, the Czechs and the Germans are the heartiest drinkers, with Belgium, Ireland and Luxembourg not far behind. Only the Australians from outside Europe are in the same league.

While the output of beer was growing, the number of working breweries fell. By 1973, there were only one-tenth of the number operating in 1873. The average brewery today is thus far larger than its 19th century counterpart, though there are exceptions. The Bavarians like to claim that they still have as many separate brewing units as the rest of the world put together. In 1952, the number was over 2,500. Britain today has less than 200 breweries.

In many countries a few large companies produce a large proportion of the beer. In Eastern Europe and much of Africa these are state-owned, while elsewhere they are often part of larger undertakings with interests in other areas of industry. Watney-Mann, one of

the "Big Six" British brewers, is owned by the Grand Metropolitan Hotels group.

Another worldwide trend in recent years has been a growing interest in beers from abroad. The insular attitude of the beer drinker has gradually faded as companies like Carlsberg and Guinness have expanded their activities to cover most countries of the world.

Carlsberg has set up breweries in areas where the growth in beer consumption has been greatest: in Africa (Malawi), Asia (Malaysia) and South America (Brazil). It also spearheaded the swift increase in lager sales in Britain in recent years, establishing its own brewery at Northampton.

The "lager revolution" in British drinking habits has been criticised for the low quality and high price of many draught lagers brewed locally. But in their wake have come a wide selection of imported lagers from Europe, America and Australia, including some of the world's most celebrated brews.

In contrast with this cosmopolitan trend among some British drinkers has been a renewed emphasis on a beer unique to this country, traditionally-brewed draught bitter. In the post-war period it had been all but phased out in favour of the more convenient keg bitter, but is now widely available again, mainly because of the skilful pressure of the Campaign For Real Ale, which now has over 20,000 members and is still growing.

Sweden
Despite the country's tough liquor controls, Sweden has 30 breweries. Alcohol can only be bought in plain brown bags at Government-owned stores.

United States
The Mid-West, where many immigrants from Northern Europe settled, is the brewing centre of America. The main brands include Schlitz, Pabst and Ballantine.

Switzerland
Hurlimann Sternbrau, a leading Swiss lager, is sold in Britain by Shepherd Neame. The country has 12 major breweries each producing over 1m. gallons per annum.

France

Although it is mainly a wine producing country, France has 40 large-scale breweries. The best lagers come from Alsace in the north-east.

Greece

Beer takes third place to retsina and ouzo among Greek drinks. Its lagers are of a high quality. Fix, the most popular, was introduced by Bavarian brewers.

Australia

Brewing is mainly in the hands of Carlton United Breweries and Swan. C.U.B. produce Foster's, while Castlemain, Toohey's and Tooths are also exported.

Finland

Although the Finns are among the lowest average consumers of alcohol in Europe, they are renowned for their drinking bouts. Finland has 14 breweries.

Malawi

The heaviest consumers of beer in Africa are to be found in countries formerly under Belgian and British rule. Malawi's main brewery is owned by Carlsberg.

Denmark

Brewing in Denmark is dominated by Carlsberg, founded in 1847 and now state-owned. There are over 50 other breweries in the country.

West Germany

The country has more breweries than anywhere else in the world, with 70 producing over 1m. gallons annually. Alpine Ayingerbrau is widely available in Northern England.

The Netherlands

Heineken dominate brewing in Holland, with 4 out of the country's 24 breweries. In Britain, Heineken lagers are manufactured under licence by Whitbread.

Belgium

The Belgians are among Europe's biggest beer drinkers. The most popular brews include the very bitter Kriek. Stella Artois is exported to Britain.

85

British beers

Only a few years ago, most connoisseurs of British beer viewed the situation with gloom and despondency. Many local breweries had been taken over and then closed down by large national companies, who then supplied the pubs with keg beers manufactured at massive, centralized modern breweries. There had also been a steady decline in the alcoholic strength of beer, due mainly to the way in which beer is taxed: the stronger the brew, the higher is the duty payable on it. Finally, the big brewers seemed likely to rid themselves of their traditional image.

Recently, however the tide has turned. The profits of the remaining small traditional breweries have soared relatively to those of the Big Six. The Big Six is a term used to describe the companies most responsible for the spate of brewery takeovers since the war. They are Allied Breweries (Ind Coope, Ansells Tetley), Bass Charrington (Mitchells & Butlers, Stones, Tennent, Welsh), Courage (John Smith), Scottish & Newcastle (Youngers, McEwan) Watney Mann (Truman, Usher, Websters, Wilsons, Drybrough) and Whitbread.

The growing number of drinkers insisting on traditional draught bitter has encouraged most of the Big Six to re-introduce draught into a considerable number of their pubs, particularly in London and the south-east.

SOME BRITISH BEERS & THEIR STRENGTHS

OG	Beer and brewery
1068.0	Adnams Broadside, Strong Pale Ale (bottle) (Southwold, Suffolk)
1066.3	Theakston's Old Peculier Strong Ale (Masham, Yorks.)
1054.5	Fuller's Extra Special Bitter (London)
1051.4	Worthington White Shield bottled beer (Burton)
1050.4	Ruddle's County Bitter (Oakham, Leics.)
1050.0	Hicks Special (St Austell, Cornwall)
1050.0	Everards Old Original (Burton)
1048.2	Greene King Abbot Ale (Bury St Edmunds, Suffolk)
1047.0	Ind Coope Draught Burton (Burton)
1046.5	Paine's EG Bitter (St Neots, Cambs.)
1045.7	Young's Special (London)
1045.0	Guinness bottled (winter) (London)
1044.2	Brickwood's Best (Portsmouth)
1044.0	Watney's Fined Bitter (Norwich)
1043.0	Courage Director's Bitter (London)
1043.1	Younger's IPA (Edinburgh)
1043.0	Brakspear's Special (Henley-on-Thames)
1042.7	Marston Pedigree (Burton)
1042.3	Vaux Samson (Sunderland)
1042.0	Adnam's Olde Ale
1042.0	Devenish Best Bitter (Redruth, Cornwall)
1042.0	Guinness bottled (summer) (London)
1041.8	Newcastle Exhibition (Newcastle upon Tyne)
1041.0	Robinson's Best Bitter (Stockport)
1040.5	Eldridge Pope IPA (Dorchester, Dorset)

1040.3 Federation Special (Newcastle upon Tyne)
1040.2 Double Diamond (Burton)
1040.2 Cameron's Strongarm (Hartlepool, Durham)
1039.9 Tetley Bitter (Leeds)
1039.8 Hall and Woodhouse Best Bitter (Blandford Forum, Dorset)
1039.4 Harvey's Best Bitter (Lewes, Sussex)
1039.4 Whitbread Best Bitter (Tiverton, Devon)
1039.3 Hartley's Bitter (Ulverston, Cumbria)
1039.3 Vaux Gold Tankard (Sunderland)
1039.0 Carrington IPA (Birmingham)
1039.0 Courage Best Bitter (Bristol)
1039.0 Welsh Brewers HB (Cardiff)
1039.0 Shepherd Neame Best Bitter (Faversham, Kent)
1038.9 Mitchell's & Butler's Brew XI (Birmingham)
1038.9 Davenports Bitter (Birmingham)
1038.8 Theakston's Best Bitter (Carlisle)
1038.8 Banks Bitter (Wolverhampton)
1038.6 Arkell's BBB (Swindon, Wilts.)
1038.3 Courage Best Bitter (Reading)
1038.3 Courage Tavern Keg (Reading)
1038.1 Ward's Bitter (Sheffield)
1037.8 Wadworth's 6X Bitter (Devizes, Wilts.)
1037.2 Whitbread Tankard (15 breweries throughout the country).
1037.2 Ind Coope Best Bitter (Burton)
1037.1 Worthington E (Burton)
1037.0 Ansell's Bitter (Birmingham)
1036.7 Hyde's Bitter (Manchester)
1036.6 Shepherd Neame Bitter (Faversham, Kent)

1036.3 Samuel Smith's Old Brewery Bitter (Tadcaster, Yorks.)
1036.2 Belhaven 70/- Ale (Dunbar, Scotland)
1036.0 Thwaites Bitter (Blackburn, Lancs.)
1036.0 Worthington E Keg Bitter (Burton)
1035.7 Ansell's Mild (Birmingham)
1035.6 Buckley's Best Bitter (Llanelli, Dyfed)
1035.5 McEwan's Best Scotch 70/- Ale (Edinburgh)
1035.5 Younger's Tartan Keg Bitter (Edinburgh)
1035.4 Boddington's Bitter (Manchester)
1035.3 Felinfoel Bitter (Llanelli, Dyfed)
1035.1 Lorimer's Best Scotch Ale (Edinburgh)
1035.1 Banks Mild (Wolverhampton)
1034.8 Whitbread Trophy (Marlow, Bucks.)
1034.8 Charles Wells Bitter (Bedford)
1034.8 Border Bitter (Wrexham, Clwyd)
1034.6 Jennings Bitter (Cockermouth, Cumbria)
1034.4 Drybrough Keg Heavy (Edinburgh)
1034.1 Tolly Cobbold Bitter (Ipswich, Suffolk)
1034.0 Matthew Brown Bitter (Blackburn, Lancs.)
1033.9 Morland PA Bitter (Abingdon, Oxon.)
1035.5 Brain's Bitter (Cardiff)
1033.0 Boddington's Mild (Manchester)
1032.8 King & Barnes PA Bitter (Horsham, Sussex)
1032.7 Greenall Whitley Mild (Warrington)
1031.2 Ushers PA (Trowbridge, Wilts.)
1031.0 Shepherd Neame Mild (Faversham, Kent)
1030.0 Adnams Mild (Southwold, Suffolk)

Sources: Good Beer Guide 1976; Sunday Mirror 25.7.76

Beer and the law

Control of licences to sell beer have traditionally been in the hands of local magistrates. It was not until 1830 that the first national regulation to restrict pub hours was passed. It has since been followed by a series of licensing laws:

1830 Pub opening hours restricted to 4 am to 10 pm.

1839 Pubs to be shut from midnight on Saturday to noon on Sunday.

1872 Magistrates' power to grant, control or transfer licences reinforced. A cheaper six-day licence (excluding Sunday) introduced as an alternative to seven-day ones.

1901 No child under 14 to be served with alcoholic liquor.

1914 The Defence Of The Realm Act, introduced at the outbreak of war, brought in the set opening hours that have lasted, with few modifications, to the present day.

1923 Minimum drinking age raised to 18.

1961 Ten minutes "drinking up time" introduced.

1975 Erroll Committee on licensing laws recommends relaxation of restrictions on opening hours, and rooms in pubs to which children may be admitted. This would bring Britain into line with most other EEC countries.

Prior to 1880, brewers paid tax to the Customs & Excise on the malt used in their beer. In that year, a new system based on the Original Gravity of unfermented wort was introduced. It has remained virtually unchanged ever since. Because duty was less on weaker beers, this method of taxation had the effect of encouraging brewers to lower the strength of their product. That, plus the compulsory reduction in strength during two World Wars, has meant that the average OG of British beer has declined from 1057 in 1880 to about 1037 today.

Inn signs

Local alehouses have always proclaimed their independence by their choice of names and by the skill and ingenuity with which their signs illustrated a national event, a local noble family's arms or a common heraldic device.

Conversion tables

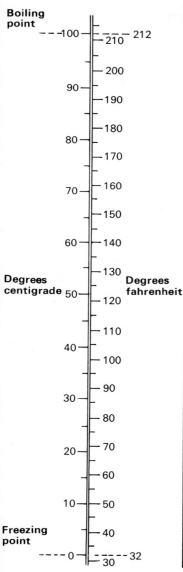

Boiling point

Degrees centigrade

Freezing point

Degrees fahrenheit

Imperial				Metric
5 gallons	=	800 fl oz	=	22.8 litres
1 gallon	=	160 fl oz	=	4.55 litres
1 quart	=	40 fl oz	=	114 centilitres
1 pint	=	20 fl oz	=	57 cl
$\frac{1}{2}$ pint	=	10 fl oz	=	28 cl
1 dessertspoon	=	$\frac{1}{3}$ fl oz	=	1 cl
1 teaspoon	=	$\frac{1}{6}$ fl oz	=	0.5 cl

Liquid measure

Metric			
1 litre	=		10 decilitres (dl) =
100 centilitres (cl)	=		1,000 millilitres (ml)

Imperial				
1 litre	=	35 fl oz	=	$1\frac{3}{4}$ pints
$\frac{1}{2}$ litre	=	$17\frac{1}{2}$ fl oz	=	$\frac{7}{8}$ pints
$\frac{1}{4}$ litre	=	$8\frac{3}{4}$ fl oz	=	$\frac{7}{16}$ pints
1 cl	=	$\frac{1}{3}$ fl oz	=	1 dessertspoon

American measures differ in that there are only 16 fl oz in a US pint, thus:

American				Metric
1 gallon	=	128 fl oz	=	3.64 litres
1 pint	=	16 fl oz	=	2 cups = 45.5 cl
1 tablespoon	=	$\frac{1}{3}$ fl oz	=	1 UK dessert spoon = 1 cl

Metric				American
1 litre	=	35 fl oz	=	$2\frac{1}{5}$ pints
1 cl	=	$\frac{1}{3}$ fl oz	=	1 tablespoon

The UK and US teaspoon are $\frac{1}{6}$ fl oz
N.B. When using a recipe book check whether it is British or American
All equivalents are necessarily approximate.

Metric		Solid measure		Imperial
1 kilo	=	1,000 grammes	=	2 lb 3 oz
$\frac{1}{2}$ kilo	=	500 grammes	=	1 lb $1\frac{1}{2}$ oz
$\frac{1}{4}$ kilo	=	250 grammes	=	9 oz
$\frac{1}{8}$ kilo	=	125 grammes	=	$4\frac{1}{2}$ oz
$\frac{1}{10}$ kilo	=	100 grammes	=	$3\frac{1}{2}$ oz

Imperial				Metric
1 lb	=	16 oz	=	454 grammes
$\frac{1}{2}$ lb	=	8 oz	=	227 grammes
$\frac{1}{4}$ lb	=	4 oz	=	113 grammes
$\frac{1}{16}$ lb	=	1 oz	=	28 grammes

Courses

Although many local authorities offer evening classes on wine-making, those on home-brewing are few and far between. If you require personal assistance, the manager of your local home brewing shop may be able to help, or there may be an amateur brewers and wine-makers circle or society in the area. The address of such a group can usually be found at the local Public Library or Citizens Advice Bureau.

For anyone wishing to take up a career in brewing, the industry has a number of training schemes for technicians, scientists and licensees. University graduates in science subjects can take a one-year post-graduate course at Birmingham or Heriot-Watt Universities. For those wishing to enter the industry straight from school, many brewery companies have training schemes involving study for various professional qualifications, including those of the Institute of Brewing.

Further details on brewing as a career can be obtained from: The Technical Secretary, The Brewers' Society, 42 Portman Square, London W1H 0BB. Tel. 01-486 4831.

ASSOCIATIONS

Campaign For Real Ale, 34 Alma Street, St. Albans, Herts. AL1 3BW. Membership fee: £2 per year. With many local branches, CAMRA exists to champion the cause of tradition-al draught bitter and to ensure its survival. It publishes the "Good Beer Guide" and many local lists of pubs serving "real ale". CAMRA Investments Ltd. owns free houses in London, Bristol, Cheshire and Leeds.

The Brewers' Society, 42 Portman Square, London W1H 0BB. The professional association of commercial breweries. It runs a research establishment at Reigate in Surrey.

British Beer Mat Collectors Society, 142 Leicester Street, Wolverhampton WV6 0PS.

Suppliers

Most large towns have a shop specializing in equipment and ingredients for the home brewer. If there is no home brewing shop in your area, the local branch of Boots the Chemist or a health food store will usually stock beer kits and other materials. In London, the most comprehensive range of equipment can be obtained from: W. R. Loftus Ltd., 1 Charlotte Street, London W1. Tel. 01-636 6235.

HOME BREW KITS

The following are among the principal manufacturers of home brew kits. If you have difficulty in obtaining their products, write to the firm for details of the nearest stockist.

Boots The Chemist, 1 Thaine Road West, Nottingham.

Cumbria Home Brews, Townfoot Industrial Estate, Brampton, Cumbria CA8 1SP.

Geordie: Viking Brews Ltd., 28/9 Clive Street, North Shields, Tyne & Wear.

Kwoffit: Itona Products Ltd., Leyland Mill Lane, Wigan, Lancashire.

Unican Foods Ltd., Unican House, Central Trading Estate, Bath Road, Bristol.

Compe-titions

Many horticultural and other shows now have sections devoted to home-brewed beer of various types. In general, the kinds of beer to be entered are described in the usual way, e.g. bitter, lager, brown ale, stout, etc. But if you decide to enter a competition, it is important to know what the judges will be looking for, and what are considered the most important aspects of a good beer.

Attention is paid first of all to the bottling of the beer. A space of not less than 1 cm ($\frac{1}{2}$ in.) should be left between the stopper and the beer itself. The bottle is required to be a brown or green one, and it and the cork will be checked for cleanliness.

More marks are awarded for the condition and clarity of the brew. This includes the firmness of the head when poured and the absence of any haziness in the beer in the glass. Any yeast deposit in the bottom of the bottle should remain there when the beer is carefully poured. The brew should also produce a steady flow of bubbles when opened. Excessive flatness is penalized in beer contests.

The bouquet of the beer is also taken into account by the judges, but the crucial factor is the taste. Although this is to some extent a subjective matter, the judges will have been chosen for their experience of large numbers of beers of each type. They will be checking that the brew is not over-acidic or too sweet, and is fresh, clean and well-balanced.

Book list

A History Of English Ale And Beer, H. A. Monckton, Bodley Head, 1966. The best general introduction to the subject, now out of print but available from public libraries.

A History Of Brewing, H. S. Corran. David & Charles, 1975, £6.50.
Deals mainly with the technical changes over the centuries, which are very clearly explained. Well illustrated.

Beer Is Best, John Watney, Peter Owen, 1974, £2.50.
A light-hearted but informative social history of British beer.

The Plain Man's Guide to Beer. C. L. Duddington, Pelham Books, 1974, £2·90.
A somewhat misleading title since the book is mainly concerned with detailed descriptions of modern commercial brewing techniques.

The Beer Drinker's Companion, Frank Baillie, David & Charles, 1973, £3.25.
A guide to the wide range of British beers and breweries by an author who has sampled most of them.

The Good Beer Guide,
Michael Hardman (editor), Arrow Books for the Campaign For Real Ale, published annually, £1.40 (1976).
Lists 4,000 pubs stocking cask-conditioned beers throughout the U.K. Keg beers are not included.

Pub Games, Arthur R. Taylor, Arrow, 1976, 95p.
The definitive guide to its subject, expertly and entertainingly written.

HOME-BREWING
Home-brewing of beer is in the unusual position of being both one of the oldest and one of the most recent crafts practised. Due to Excise restrictions up to 1963, brewing alcoholic beverages in one's own home was forbidden by law.

Since the restrictions were lifted, an abundance of books on home-brewing have come on to the market. Some of the more comprehensive are:

Brewing Better Beers, Ken Shales, Amateur Winemaker, 1967, 35p.
A light-hearted but accurate guide to brewing both for the beginner and the more advanced brewer. Emphasis put on malt extract beers.

Advanced Home-Brewing,
Ken Shales, Amateur Winemaker, 1972, 40p.
The second book by this widely read author. As the title suggests, this was written for the practising brewer and so is best read in conjunction with the above book.

The Big Book of Brewing,
Dave Line, Amateur Winemaker, 1974, 75p.
Certainly the most comprehensive book on the subject, and essential reading for all enthusiastic brewers. Emphasis on all-grain beers.

Home Brewed Beers and Stouts, C. J. J. Berry, Amateur Winemaker, 1968, 35p.
This was the first book published on home-brewing following its legalisation. The easy to follow layout has made this one of the most popular guides for the beginner.

Home Brewing Without Failures, H. E. Bravery, Macdonald, 1965, 95p.
Also published soon after legalization. Although mainly dealing with beer, the author also has included helpful sections on mock beers, cider and mead.

Beer Making for All,
J. Macgregor, Faber, 1967, £1.40. A well written book and one which acknowledges the importance of understanding the technique of brewing before trying out recipes.

PERIODICALS

What's Brewing, Campaign For Real Ale, 34 Alma Street, St. Albans, Herts. AL1 3BW. 10p monthly. The official journal of CAMRA, it includes articles on many subjects of general interest to the beer-drinker, including home-brewing. Free to CAMRA members.

Brewing Review, Brewing Publications Ltd., 42 Portman Square, London W1H 0BB. Monthly, 45p single copies. Annual subscription £5.00. The official journal of the Brewers' Society which contains information on the latest developments in commercial brewing at home and abroad.

Brewers' Guardian,
Northwood Publications Ltd., 93-99 Goswell Road, London EC1V 7QA. Single copies 65p. Annual subscription £7.00. Covers the same area as Brewing Review but is independent of the industry.

Home Beer & Winemaking,
Foremost Press Ltd., P.O. Box No. 1, Wirral, Merseyside L46 0TS. 20p monthly. Annual subscription £4.00. A good source of recipes and advice, with a large advertising section containing details of equipment and ingredients.

Glossary

Adjuncts: unmalted grain starches, normally in "flaked" form, which are added to the grist to supplement the fermentable extract. Some also contribute flavour. Their addition in high-gravity beers can prevent the occurrence of hazing. Commercially, adjuncts are often used in high proportions, being a more economical source of extract.

Attemperation: the process by which the temperature of the wort is controlled at various stages of brewing. Commercially, this is done by installing pipes through which hot or cold water can be run inside the vats.

Attenuation: the lowering of specific gravity of a beer during fermentation. The density of the liquid declines as the sugar content in solution is converted into equal proportions of carbon dioxide gas and alcohol.

Bine: the climbing stem of the hop plant on which the flowers grow.

Brewers' yeast: the strain of yeast, also termed *Saccharomyces cerevisiae,* which is used for top-fermenting beers. Produces a yeast head which remains on the surface during primary fermentation.

Carbonation: the name given to modern methods of bottling and kegging beer in which extra carbon dioxide is added to commercial beers not naturally conditioned to prevent flatness in the finished beer.

Carbon dioxide: the gas produced, along with alcohol, by the reaction of yeast and sugar during fermentation.

Cold break: precipitation of protein matter from the wort during the rapid cooling period prior to fermentation

Condition: this refers to the "life" a beer has due to the amount of carbon dioxide gas in it. The pressure, so formed, is released when exposed to air. "Naturally conditioned" beers are those where the gas content has been produced from yeast and priming sugar in the bottle or cask.

Copper: the vessel in which the wort is boiled before being fermented, now usually made of stainless steel.

Dextrin: one of the two sugars produced during mashing. Converted from starch by the enzyme alpha amylase. Has a retarded reaction with yeast and is taken up during secondary fermentation (see maltose).

Dry hopping: a method of replacing some of the flavour of the hops lost during boiling. The additional hops or hop oils are added loose to the beer 48 hours before bottling.

Enzymes: the chemical catalysts which cause the transformation of the starch in the malt into sugars suitable for fermentation.

Fermentation: the final stage of beer-making in which the action of yeast causes the conversion of the sugars in the wort into alcohol and carbon dioxide.

Filtration: with fining, a widely used method of clarifying the finished beer in commercial brewing. The filters extract any remaining impurities or sediment after fermentation.

Finings: substances added to beer after brewing. They act to clear the brew of suspended solids. Isinglass, the swim bladder of the sturgeon, and Irish Moss are widely used as finings.

Fobbing: the fobbing or foaming of beer occurs either from over-priming, over-filling or from storage at too high a temperature. This results in excessive gas content which must be liberated with caution.

Gibberellic acid: a chemical substance added to the malt to speed up the production of enzymes and thus cut down the malting time. Used in commercial brewing.

Grist: the mixture of barley malt and adjuncts which forms the basis of the wort.

Hot break: the coagulation of fine protein particles into flocculating matter. This "hot break" is achieved after approximately one hour of boiling.

Hydrometer: the instrument used to measure the original gravity of the wort.

Irish Moss: also known as "Copper finings". A fining agent prepared from two types of seaweed, which precipitates protein matter out of solution at the boiling stage. Mainly for use with light-coloured beers.

Lager yeasts: *(Saccharomyces Carlsbergenis).* This is a pure strain of yeast which is also called a bottom fermenter. Primarily used with lagers, this yeast works best in anaerobic conditions under air-lock.

Liquor: the brewer's term for any water used in the making of beer.

Malt: barley grains whose germination has been artificially induced to convert their starch content into sugars suitable for fermentation.

Malt extract: concentrated malt wort either produced in syrup form or powdered. When brewing with a mixture of malt extract and grain, a diastatic malt extract must be used in order to convert the additional starch.

Maltose: one of the two sugars produced during mashing. Converted from starch by the enzyme beta amylase. Reacts rapidly with yeast during primary fermentation (see dextrin).

Mashing: the treatment of the grist by mixing it with hot water to extract its active ingredients in solution. The resulting liquid is the wort.

Mash tun: the name given to the container used in mashing.

Maturation: the period, after racking, during which the finished beer is stored, for impurities to settle out and, with live beers, for a secondary fermentation to occur.

Original gravity (OG): The density of the liquid, and thus its potential alcohol content as measured prior to fermentation. See "Specific gravity".

Pasteurization: the heating of finished beer for a very short time to destroy any remaining bacteria. This method is generally used with bottled beers in commercial brewing.

Pitching: the addition of yeast to the wort so that fermentation can begin.

Priming: the addition of sugar to beer in order to produce a final fermentation in the bottle or cask. Beer treated in this way is "naturally conditioned"

Racking: siphoning beer off the sediment in one container into a fresh container.

Rousing: the vigorous stirring during primary fermentation that aerates the brew. Rousing should "roll" the beer from bottom to top in a circular motion.

Sediment: the deposits of yeast and insoluble solids that settle out during fermentation and storage. Also is referred to as grounds, lees and bottoms.

Skimming: the removal of surplus yeast and unwanted matter from the top of the yeast head during the first stage of fermentation.

Sparging: the spraying of the spent matter after mashing to extract any remaining fermentable material.

Specific gravity: The means of assessing the alcohol potential of beer by measuring the relative density of a sugary solution to that of water.

Steeping: the soaking of barley grains in water to begin the malting process.

Strike heat: the temperature of the liquor immediately before mixing it with the grist for mashing.

Wort: the term used to describe the malt solution from the time it is collected from the mashed grain up until fermentation.

Yeast bite: used to describe a harsh taste in beer. Normally caused by using a poor or incorrect strain of yeast. Beer with a yeast haze will have this distinctive flavour as can beer left for too long over a thick sediment.

Index

Credits

Artists
Ron Hayward Art Group
Vanessa Luff
Q E D
John Shackell

Photographs
The Bettman Archive:
Contents, 24
Brewers' Research Foundation:
    12
The Brewers' Society:
    Contents, 14, 15, 41, 88
The British Museum: 8
Mary Evans Picture Library:
    Contents, 7, 19, 23
Paul Forrester: 21, 29, 37, 44,
    52, 58, 69, 76
Guinness: 15
Keystone Press: 13
Picturepoint: 5, 12

Radio Times Hulton Picture
    Library: 11, 23, 71
Ronan Picture Library: 6, 9,
    10, 38, 57
Whitbread: 20
Vallery Wilmer: 27, 36, 42, 45,
    46, 53, 55, 62
Young & Co.: 18, 43, 56
Zefa: 25

Cover
Design: Design Machine
Photograph: Paul Forrester